A Festival of
DRESSAGE

A Festival of
DRESSAGE

JANE KIDD

HOWELL BOOK HOUSE INC.
230 Park Avenue, New York, N.Y. 10169

Published 1986 by Howell Book House, Inc.
230 Park Avenue, New York, NY 10169

First published in 1981 in Great Britain by Stanley Paul & Co. Ltd
Copyright © Inchcape & Co. Ltd 1981

Library of Congress Cataloging-in-Publication Data

Kidd, Jane.
  A festival of dressage.
  1. International Dressage Championship, Goodwood,
West Sussex. 2. Dressage tests. I. Title.
SF309.6.K5 1986   798.2'3   86–10575
ISBN 0–87605–859–4

Designed by Jonathan Gill-Skelton
Computerset in Zapf International by
MFK Graphic Systems (Typesetting) Ltd
Saffron Walden, Essex
Colour separation by Fotographics Ltd
Printed and bound in Great Britain by Butler & Tanner Ltd

CONTENTS

AUTHOR'S NOTE

I should like to thank the two international judges, Mrs Joan Gold and Mrs Sheila Inderwick for the advice they have given me in preparing this book. It has been a difficult job – dressage is often criticized for being too complicated. Consequently, in trying to simplify it I have had to gloss over some technical points, not cover every aspect and, for the experts, perhaps appear superficial. This is particularly the case in the commentaries on the photographs. The pictures catch a fleeting moment in a long series of actions. I have been bold enough to give my subjective impression of some of the features of that fleeting moment because I would like more people to understand more about what is good and bad in dressage. Some might interpret that moment differently or have pointed out other features. Absolute judgements are difficult to make without seeing what has happened before or after. This is especially so in a sport in which absolute values are tempered by artistic licence.

FOREWORD

Dressage, although a highly specialized equestrian activity, is now attracting more participants than ever before. Its increasing popularity is reflected in the continuing success of the International Dressage Championship which has taken place at Goodwood over the last nine years. This international competition – the only one to be held in Britain – attracts the world's top dressage riders, and also provides an unique opportunity for young riders and horses to take part in special events.

Since 1979 the Inchcape Group have been sponsors of this competition. The Inchcape Group is proud to further the interests of dressage through sponsorship of this book.

INTRODUCTION

History of dressage

Dressage is simply the training of the horse – training him to use his body with the suppleness and control of a gymnast, the grace and lightness of a ballet dancer. It is a fascinating experience for a rider to develop these abilities in a horse. He has to find ways of being understood by the horse, of mastering the techniques which supple and develop the muscles the horse needs to perform the increasingly difficult movements, and he has to win his co-operation and respect so that they can work together in harmony.

The goal in dressage is that tantalizing one of perfect performance, but although rarely achieved there are great moments of exhilaration and satisfaction, such as when a horse suddenly grasps what his rider wants, or tries his utmost stretching for a wonderful rhythmic extension, or springs powerfully with each step of the passage, or compresses his body to jump nimbly around in a pirouette. When the horse is working 'with', not 'for', his rider, has achieved a harmony with him, and can perform movements that demand great athleticism, then dressage is a source of great excitement and of wonderful memories.

Right Frederico Grisone, whose riding academy in Naples became the centre of High School riding and led the revival of dressage in the sixteenth century.

Above Part of the Parthenon frieze. It shows horses in very collected positions, proving that dressage was practised in this Classical era.

L'AVANT MAIN

Le Front 1
Les Temples 2
Les Salieres 3
La Ganache 4
Les Levres 5
Les Naseaux 6
Le Bout-du-nez 7
Le Menton 8
La Barbe 9
L'Encolure 10
Le Crin ou la Criniere 11
Le Toupet 12
Le Gosier 13
Le Garot 14
Les Epaules 15
Le Poitrail 16
Le Coude 17
Le Bras 18
L'Ars 19
La Chataigne 20
Le Genou 21
Le Canon 22
Le Nerf 23
Le Boulet 24
Le Fanon 25
Le Paturon 26
La Couronne 27
Le Sabot 28
Les Quartiers 29
La Pince 30
Le Talon 31

LE CORPS

Les Reins 32
Les Rognons 33
Les Cotez 34
Le Ventre 35
Les Flancs 36

L'ARRIERE-MAIN

La Croupe 37
Le Tronçon de la Queue 38
Les Fesses 39
Les Hanches 40
Le Grasset 41
Les Cuisses 42
Le Jarret 43
La Chataigne 44
La Pointe du Jarret 45

Above Illustrations from *L'Ecole de Cavalerie*, a book published in 1736 and written by probably the greatest riding master of all time, the Frenchman François de la Guérinière.

The fun of training the horse is not a new discovery. It is likely that man tried very early in history, in a rudimentary manner, to train horses, for by the Classical era the Greeks had become great dressage riders. They left proof in the forms of the Parthenon frieze, showing horses performing complicated movements, and the literature of Xenophon, the first great writer on horsemanship.

The Romans, who sought more basic pleasures, concentrated their equestrian interests on such sports as chariot-racing. The aesthetic lure of dressage, requiring great discipline of horse and rider, did not appeal. For centuries riders asked for little more control over their horses than stopping, accelerating and turning quickly.

It was in the age of the Renaissance, in the spirit of a time when classical literature and art were reborn, and interest in culture revived, that dressage was re-established as an important activity. An academy was founded in Naples in 1532 by the Neapolitan nobleman Frederico Grisone. Horsemasters experimented with different ways of teaching horses to perform intricate and spectacular movements.

Above An eighteenth-century illustration of travers, a movement which is still used in dressage tests today.

Above During the nineteenth century one of the most popular outlets for dressage training was the circus. In this engraving two Russian horses can be seen performing in liberty.

Young noblemen flocked there to learn the techniques of this art of High School, which rapidly became the craze at courts all over Europe. It was a fashion that did not die out, although the centre was transferred from Italy to France in the late sixteenth century.

For three hundred years the aristocrats on the Continent spent most of their time on horseback, learning how to make horses go sideways, to leap in the air on command and to show off these activities in extravagant equestrian pageants and carousels; the British, on the other hand, much preferred to gallop in pursuit of hounds or the winning post on a racecourse. The Continentals were the equestrian artists, the British the equestrian sportsmen.

Riding masters on the Continent, many of whom became court favourites, gradually evolved a logical series of steps of converting the untrained horse into an equine gymnast over a period of three or four years. Fortunately they discovered, too, that any reluctance to perform the complicated movements was not due to truculence and disobedience, which they would attempt to cure with sharp spurs, a long whip and atrociously severe bits, but to a lack of ability and of muscle development, and a failure to understand. Gradually the horsemasters of Europe found ways of training horses by encouraging co-operation rather than threatening punishment.

These methods have changed little over the last hundred years, but what *has* changed is the outlet for the training. Whereas the end-products of dressage training were used in public displays, including the circus, they are now, in line with the modern fashion, used to compete against others. Twentieth-century dressage has more followers treating it as a competitive sport than as a form of display.

Above The Spanish Riding School is the most famous and important custodian of the art of dressage. This is a dramatic picture of the courbette, one of the airs above the ground (none of which is included in today's dressage tests).

This development was spurred on by the restoration in 1896 of the Olympic Games. Riders were reinstated as permanent Olympians in the 1912 Stockholm Games, but the dressage was more of a test of obedience than of gymnastic ability and training. Participants' control over their horses was tested by having to pass strange objects, and only relatively simple movements (e.g. extensions and collection) were included.

As with other sports, participation at the Olympic Games became such an all-consuming goal for athletes that standards rose rapidly; the dressage tests became more and more difficult (piaffe and passage were first asked for at the 1936 Games). Today, perfect or even near-perfect execution of the movements included in the international tests is an impossibility. Today's greats can at best hope for a 70 per cent final mark.

The Continentals took up dressage competitions with much the same enthusiasm as they had had for displays at court. In Germany, France, Switzerland and Sweden, in particular, the dressage became as popular as show-jumping and eventing. The English, however, continued to treat it as a mystical activity only suitable for those who did not enjoy the excitements of jumping fences. The odd rider did take it up seriously, but the most successful spent a good deal of time on the Continent. Joan Gold, Britain's first winner of an international Grand Prix (1958, in Aachen), spent many years in Germany as an army officer's wife, and Yook Hall, who won three Hamburg Derbies and three Grand Prix between 1960 and 1968 for Britain, was born and brought up in Holland. Britain's two 'grand dames' of dressage, Mrs Brenda Williams (eleventh in the 1960 Games) and Mrs Lorna Johnstone (twelfth in the 1972 Games), trained in England but were influenced by Continental instructors.

Above Mrs Lorna Johnstone and El Farruco training at the rider's home. This pair had the distinction of coming twelfth at the Munich Olympics in 1972.

Above An early British dressage representative, Mrs Brenda Williams (61), at the 1956 Stockholm Olympic Games. Her horse Pilgrim was then 19.

Goodwood

One of the most significant steps in Britain's conversion to this artistic sport was in 1973 when a major international contest was staged in Britain. The dressage-starved English were given a chance to see some of the best – a team of top Germans. The stage for this important step was Goodwood – the home of the Duke of Richmond and an estate already steeped in equestrian history. Over a period of nearly three hundred years it has played a leading rôle in increasing the popularity of two major equestrian sports – fox-hunting and racing.

The original Goodwood house was bought in 1697 by the first Duke of Richmond (the natural son of racing's great promoter Charles II). He wanted a hunting lodge, as the local Charlton Hunt was the first formal fox-hunt in Britain; and the nobility, including King William, were flocking south to participate in this new sport. In the late seventeenth century and early eighteenth century the Charlton Hunt was as prestigious and as popular as the Quorn Hunt is today.

The second Duke became Master of the Charlton but he renamed it the Goodwood Hunt. The third Duke built kennels for the hounds which were so luxurious that the hounds enjoyed a primitive form of central heating. Then the horses were given homes in stables designed by Sir William Chambers, and these were of such magnificence that they are today a Schedule 1 historic building. Finally the Duke decided

Above The first Duke of Richmond came to Goodwood in 1697, having bought a hunting lodge there.

Above Goodwood House today.

Above The third Duke of Richmond and the Charlton Hunt in a painting by George Stubbs. Fox hunting was the first equestrian activity for which Goodwood was famed.

Above Racing was Goodwood's second major equestrian activity, beginning in 1801. This print shows the Goodwood Cup taking place in 1845.

Above The annual race meeting in July at Goodwood developed into a very elegant occasion. High society flocked there in their most glamorous apparel, as depicted here in the *Illustrated London News* of 1884.

to house his family in a comparable style to that of the animals, and at the end of the eighteenth century a grandiose octagonal building with a tower at each corner was planned under the direction of James Wyatt.

Britain's main hunting interests had been transferred to Leicestershire during the eighteenth century but another sport kept Goodwood to the forefront of the equestrian world. In 1801 the third Duke ran some races for the local militia, the very first having conditions rather different from today's. It was for £50 Hunter's Plate with two-mile heats, and the seven runners were ridden by 'gentlemen' who had to carry seventeen stones.

The inaugural meeting was such a success that the Goodwood races became an annual occasion. Then in the 1830s Goodwood's racing escalated into a major event under the aegis of racing's great reformer, Lord George Bentinck. The name 'Glorious Goodwood' caught on after a journalist described one of these early events as 'the most glorious meeting

that ever man attended'. From then until the present day Goodwood has maintained a reputation for efficient organization, the natural beauty of the forum and stylish entertainments.

These are just the features which suit the staging of dressage, so when Goodwood turned its hand to promoting this Continental activity, it had the approach and the physical environment to do it well. Like the racing, dressage was an immediate success, and just five years after holding that experimental international meeting on the lawns in front of the house, Goodwood was the stage for the 1978 World Championships. In that short space of time Goodwood had become, for dressage riders, probably the most popular showground in the world.

The Festivals

When in 1980 the Russians marched into Afghanistan and Western governments asked their athletes to show their abhorrence of this act by boycotting the Moscow Olympics, it was, interestingly enough, the riders more than any other sector of athletes who rallied behind the call and were willing to sacrifice their ultimate ambition of participating in the Games. So universal was the riders' boycott that it became feasible to stage alternative equestrian games at which the standard would far surpass that of the Moscow event. The equestrian Games at Moscow were a fiasco but the Festivals (as the alternatives were named) were not.

Stages were sought that could provide the best facilities and instant organization. Rotterdam was chosen for the show-jumpers, Fontainebleau for the eventers and Goodwood for the dressage riders. Large sums of money were needed to bring together the world's top riders and provide essential facilities. At Goodwood it was the British government and Inchcape & Co Ltd who made it possible to compensate the riders for sacrificing their greatest ambition.

Top Goodwood House in the mid-nineteenth century. **Above** Dressage is the most recent addition to Goodwood's equestrian activities. This painting by J. Coleman commemorates the World Dressage Championships of 1978.

THE ARRIVAL

An aura of hushed excitement, of anxious anticipation, surrounds an international show when the competitors start to arrive. The friendly greetings, multi-lingual wisecracks and anecdotes, reflect the camaraderie of such gatherings and help to mask the taut nerves. This, at last, is the occasion for which the competitors have trained over many years. Can they make the most of it? Can they be equal to this great test? And if not capable of winning, can they at least perform well enough not to let down the relations, trainers and grooms whose support has helped them get this far? The time (three or four years spent training a particular horse, and many more years spent training themselves), the effort (the discipline

Above The horses are well-protected for their journey. Although Marco Polo only came a short distance he still wore leg- and knee-protectors.

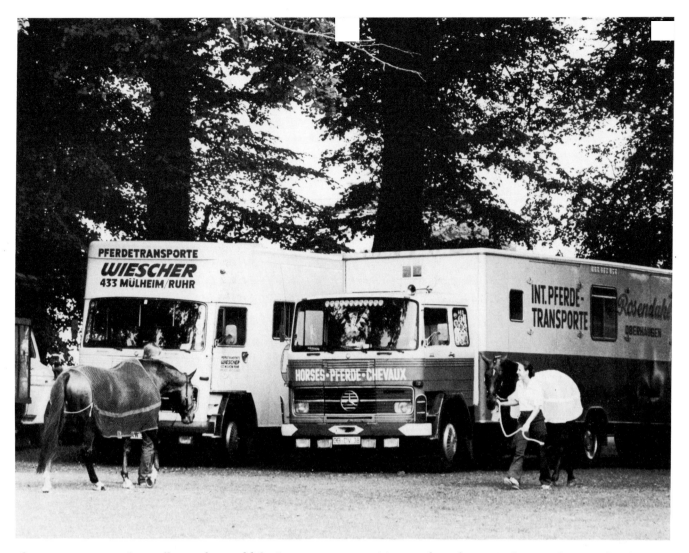

Above Horses come from all over the world for important competitions such as the Festival. Some fly to England, others come in luxurious articulated lorries like these from Germany.

of dressage, which needs daily devotion and meticulous attention to detail) and the money (the buying, training and upkeep of the horses, and the journey to the competition): all these will only seem worthwhile if, in the following few days, they can perform up to, or above, their normal standard.

This is the basis of that aura of tension surrounding even the horses as they are led out of the vehicles that carried them to the venue – anything from huge, luxurious Mercedes horseboxes from Germany, to odd, somewhat ancient, trailers (probably from Britain). The horses' temporary homes at the 1980 Festival were the historic eighteenth-century looseboxes at Goodwood. But would the animals settle mentally? Could they overcome the strains of the trying journey? Dressage horses, like ballet dancers and gymnasts, need to loosen up daily – especially those of their muscles which have been stretched and developed far more than those of other types of horse. The long hours cooped up in small spaces can have disastrous stiffening effects.

Those horses which had come to Goodwood from America, Canada and Australia had spent hours in crates and endured the extreme changes of tempera-

ture that are part of long aeroplane journeys for animals. The Continental visitors from Belgium, Denmark, France, Germany, Holland and Switzerland had it a little easier, but there was still the rough jolting during long hours spent on the road. There were frequent frustrating delays of up to twenty-four hours at the borders, where officials can be extraordinarily suspicious and inconsiderate towards equine travellers; and then the Channel crossing, before arriving at the comparative serenity of 'Glorious Goodwood'.

The Swiss team had taken no chances, coming to England a week before the Festival and then working at a temporary base. They had good reason to be serious for their team included Christine Stückelberger and Granat, the hot favourites for the individual title. This combination had achieved more than any other in the history of dressage, winning an individual Olympic Gold medal, a World Championship and two European Championships. Granat, however, was a venerable fifteen years old, and his ageing muscles must have stiffened all too easily on long journeys. An extra week in England was a sensible precaution.

Granat and Stückelberger needed to be in top form if they were to beat off the challenge posed by the leading dressage nation of Germany. Three members of the German team were possible individual contenders. There was the Swiss pair's old rivals, the tall, 26-year-old doctor Uwe Schulten-Baumer and his massive Hanoverian, Slibowitz, runners-up in the 1978 and 1979 Championships. There was the consistent farmer Uwe Sauer and his elegant Trakehner Hirtentraum, and, most competitive of all, the great champion (1973 European, 1974 World and multi-Olympic medallist) Dr Reiner Klimke, who had produced yet another international star in the 9-year-old Ahlerich.

These were the favourites, but there were some exciting young stars like Frances Verbeek-van Rooy from Holland, who had burst on the international scene with a 4th in Aachen's Grand Prix, and Anne Jensen from Denmark on the Grand Prix fledgling, the 7-year-old home-bred Marzog. Among the French contestants who were likely to give pleasing performances were Christian Carde with his elegant chestnut Solitaire, and Madame Otto Crépin with Don Giovanni; and Britain had her first real international champions in the World Bronze medallists Jennie Loriston-Clarke and Dutch Courage.

These competitors were under pressure to excel and to win the honours. Others were under pressure to do better than before. For every competitor at the Festival there was the thrill of simply competing on such an occasion and the camaraderie of international sport, but these were combined with tension – the responsibility of representing a country. The next few days would also show whether or not they could succeed in making a mark on the world of international dressage.

Above An enormous amount of equipment is needed for each horse at the competitions. Here part of Dutch Courage's gear is being wheeled to a storage area.

Above The historic Goodwood stables.

Above After a long journey the horses need to relax. Granat, the champion from Switzerland, is being given some grass by his trainer Georg Vahl.

THE PREPARATION

Dressage is a sport in which competitors pursue the unobtainable 100 per cent mark; to get close to this meticulous attention to detail, as well as ability, is vital. Marks may be unobtainable because of a lack of talent, experience or technique, but they must not be thrown away.

If there is a slip in the preparation then it can cause a horse to feel uncomfortable, make a muscle painful to use, or simply create a less than pleasing picture to the judge's eyes, all of which can waste marks. Successful dressage riders are perfectionists who take care that every detail is correct. Show-

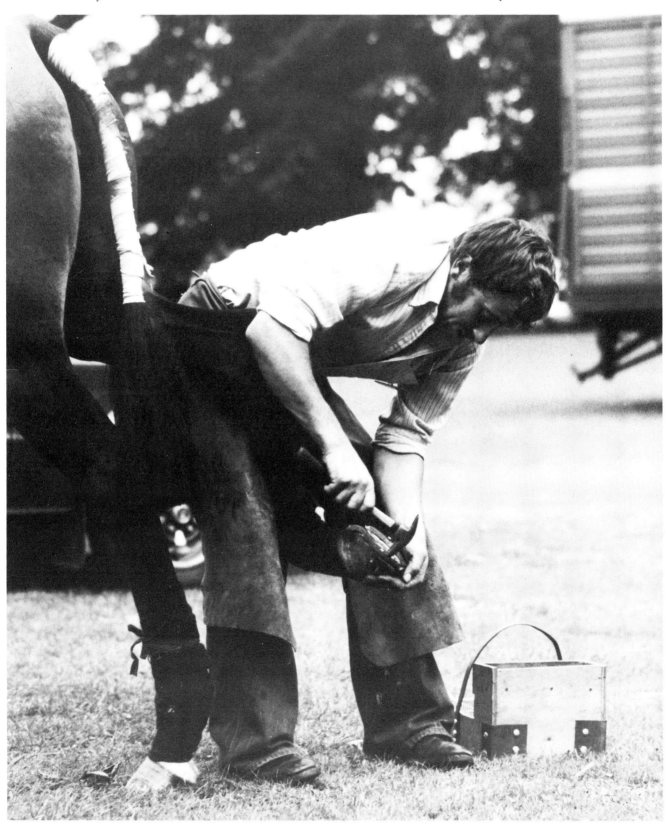

Above An important part of the preparations is shoeing. Just like human beings, horses cannot move well unless their feet are feeling comfortable.

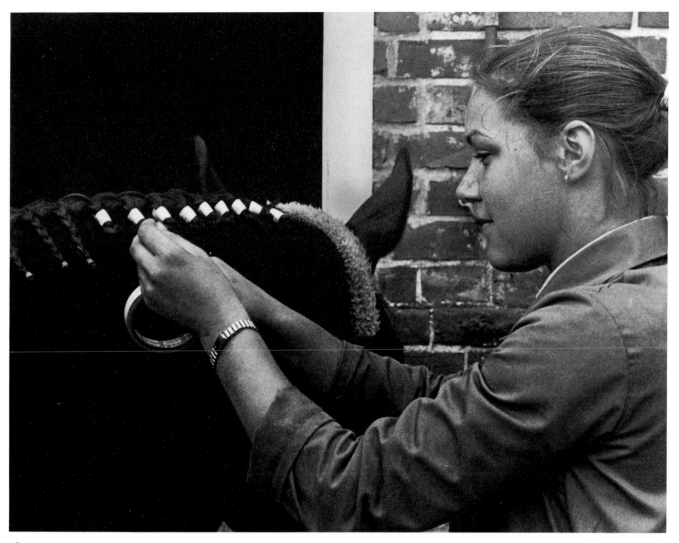

Above A well-braided mane is a vital aspect of turnout. There are many styles but in Europe this is the most popular, with white tape providing the finishing touch.

jumpers often consider the approach finicky, but if they knock a fence down it is usually considered bad luck; if a dressage rider has a poor score he has all too often lost marks through careless preparation.

The attention to detail starts with skilful horse-mastership (care in the stable). Shoes must fit and be of the right weight to enable the horse to move to the best of his ability. The feed must give him sufficient energy and good condition without making him uncontrollably high-spirited. Top dressage horses usually need as many oats as racehorses. They have to be exceptionally fit in order to develop the required muscles, to produce the vital power and forward momentum, and to work to the maximum of their ability for the ten or so minutes of the test. (In show-jumping rounds last less than two minutes, and even the Grand National is completed in less than nine minutes.)

Horses need to be well-groomed, for thorough grooming tones up the muscles and makes the animal feel good and look clean. Some competitors go so far as to use forms of physiotherapy like faradic treatment (electrical impulses at timed intervals) to keep the muscles in shape.

The saddlery is, of course, a vital consideration, but not just because it should look good on the horse. Problems such as an ill-fitting bit, the wrong type of bit, a brow band too tight, a saddle that rubs slightly, are annoying for any horse, but in dressage they create mark-losing deficiencies such as resistance in the mouth and stiffening of the back.

The general appearance is much more important than in other equestrian activities. A horse and rider turned out immaculately, with everything gleaming and in place, must feel more proud of themselves, more able to show off in the arena, than a scruffier combination would. Moreover, it must be hard for a judge not to give the odd extra mark to the combination which looks proud and pleases his eye. Dressage is a form of theatre and, as such, competitors need to show off and to look as beautiful as nature will allow.

The stables at a dressage show are a busy place. Each groom vies with the others to have his horse shining more than his neighbour's, to put in more plaits or use a more glamorous style of braiding (some use thread, others braid with white tape). Hooves have to be oiled, saddlery must be soft and clean and every inch of brass must gleam brightly.

Riders must polish their high black boots and brush their expensive tail coats. The ladies spend hours perfecting the most becoming hairstyle, to be largely hidden under dressage's pint-sized version of the top hat.

For the riders, the preparations are the straightforward part of competing, an aspect of dressage requiring no talent, just painstaking attention to detail. The final dressing-up is usually completed fairly automatically, allowing the rider's mind to dwell on other matters. It is during these preparations that the dreamers may wonder about what could occur in the dressage arena and about the glories of being in the prize-giving; the efficient riders go over, again and again, the points they must remember (to collect more before the half pass, to keep the weight more to the left in the left pirouette, to correct quickly any crookedness in that extended right canter down the longside); and the nervous ones tremble, wanting to get on with the riding, to end this tense preparation period as soon as possible.

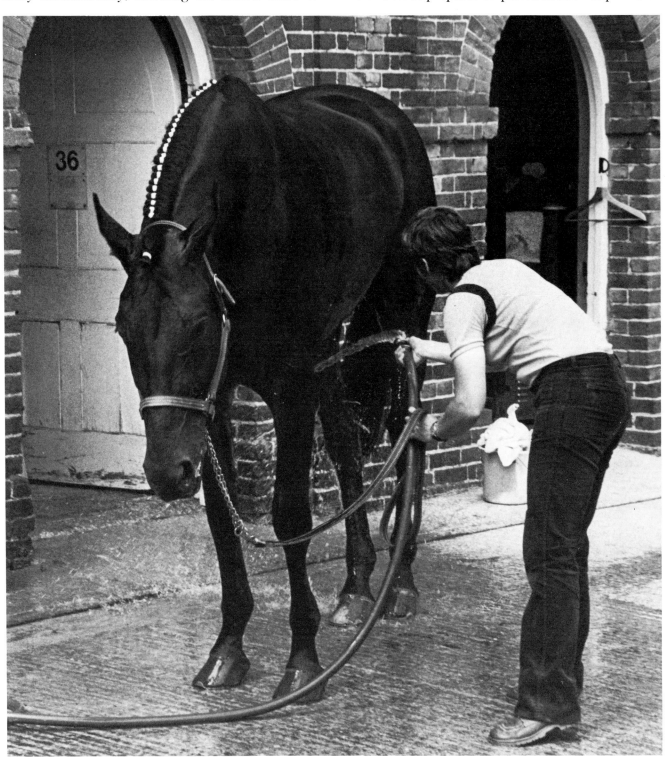

Above A final hose-down before the competition.

Above The tail also has to look neat, and a bandage is used to ensure that the hair at the top of the tail lies in place.

Above After the preparation, the riding-in must begin. This Canadian rider is passing out of the Goodwood stables under its magnificent archway.

Horse and rider ride-in to bring their abilities to the highest possible peak prior to the test in the arena. It is a fascinating process and dressage connoisseurs spend more time on the edge of the practice arena studying how it is done than watching the finished product in the test arena.

Every horse and rider needs different methods and times, and one of the most important aspects of successful competing is to be able to work out the best method of riding-in.

The four major factors to be taken into account are the mentality and the physique of the horse and the mentality and physique of the rider. The latter has to limber up as much as the horse; many riders do exercises before getting into the saddle and then ride without stirrups. Both these methods help the rider to get 'deep' into the saddle – an essential factor if he is to make the most of his horse's ability. When he is 'deep' in the saddle he can remain in the correct position and will appear to be part of the horse. He does not move from the saddle, despite the action of the horse which, especially at the sitting trot and canter, can really bump the rider. The only possible way of achieving this is for the rider to have a very

supple lower back which can move backwards and forwards and up and down along with the horse's action – hence the need for limbering up.

The rider has more to do than loosen himself up: he has to overcome any competition nerves, and to control his mind so that it is devoid of any interests other than finding ways of making his horse perform at his best. It is this ability to concentrate, to think with the horse and thus anticipate problems, which distinguishes a great competitor. Many talented riders lack it and therefore never prove their true ability in an arena; but for those who have it, it is rarely switched on at an instant. As the riding-in proceeds, that mental link with the horse becomes more and more definite, and gradually all thoughts other than how to ride 'that' horse and 'that' test are pushed out of the mind.

For the horse, the mental and physical factors are interconnected. Until he settles mentally he cannot be supple, and until he feels relaxed and supple there tend to be mental pressures. The rider has to tackle the two aspects together and decide whether the initial riding-in is best done on the lunge, free from the restriction of the rider; walking quietly away from

Above When this photograph was taken, the mist still hung over Goodwood House, but the riders start work in the practice arenas soon after 6 a.m.; they are not allowed in the international arena until the test itself.

Above The horses must be worked on the days before the competitions. Lady Inchcape on Hanalei Bay is seen here receiving help from her trainer, the Rumanian-born, German-based Georg Theodorescu.

Above The piaffe (trotting on the spot) is a movement in which the trainer's help is needed more than in any other. The horse must be encouraged to place his hindlegs well under his body and to lift them actively.

Above Mrs Judith MacKay and Debonair made the longest trip to the Festival, flying over from Australia. After such a long journey much suppling up is needed and on this occasion they were out training at the crack of dawn.

the showground; riding for an extra session early in the morning, after which the horse has time to rest; or plunging straight into the work immediately before the test. The rider will have experimented to find which method settles the horse but does not wear him out, and which exercises make him supple without using up too much energy. Regardless of methods, it is a long process. To prepare for these great tests most riders ride-in for one to two hours, and one British competitor, the ex-steeplechaser Chris Bartle, had his excitable Wily Trout ridden-out on four separate occasions in one day.

The riding-in is a piece of theatre, the dramatic conversion of the often stiff and rather heavy horse that emerges from the stables into a light, mobile, supple creature ready to perform at his best. In the early stages of the work even Grand Prix stars may look like novices. They walk, trot and canter around in an uncollected, relaxed manner performing simple serpentines and transitions. Gradually the pressure is put on, the rider applies his driving aids to make the horse more active, the hindquarters more engaged, the forehand lighter and the outline shorter, all of which make him more able to extend and collect his paces. The horse is soon asked for a little lateral work (moving sideways) and this, together with the frequent transitions within paces from collected to extended, and from one pace to another, start to make the horse's muscles increasingly supple. He becomes more manoeuvrable, more receptive and more beautiful.

The pressure really starts when the rider is ready to ask for the most advanced movements. For these, obedience is not enough: his horse must be supple, able to compress his body like a spring and so contain the power needed for the movements. The pirouettes, the piaffe, the passage and the changes all have to be practised and perfected before facing the arena. This takes time and effort and so as not to use up the horse's energy most riders give their mounts frequent breaks, even returning them to the stables for a quick clean-up and rest. But they cannot stop for long; those warmed and loosened muscles quickly freeze and become stiff again if left inactive.

Above This is the greatest trainer-pupil partnership in the dressage world – Georg Vahl from Austria and Christine Stückelberger from Switzerland. Together they have made Granat into the most successful horse in the history of dressage competitions.

Top The movement which Granat can usually perform better than any other horse is the half pass. He is taking long strides with an enormous degree of lateral action. **Above** Granat's extended trot is excellent. He is clearly showing the moment of suspension.

Above When the horses are fresh at the beginning of the riding-in they are often high-spirited and not always submissive. Ahlerich is giving Dr Reiner Klimke a difficult time.

Above The main practice arena is seen here being used for riding-in.

Above A second practice arena is available at Goodwood so that there is plenty of room for the riding-in. Many of the spectators enjoy watching the preparations for the test as much as the test itself.

Above Riding-in entails preparing the rider as well as the horse. The great German rider Reiner Klimke has taken his stirrups away to help him sit in the saddle with suppleness and balance, without relying on the irons for support. He is receiving advice from the German Chef d'Equipe and 1972 individual Olympic gold medallist Liselot Linsenhoff.

The trainer

During this gradual build-up, most riders rely on a trainer to achieve top performance. If, for example, a dressage rider turns out one foot more than another it means his seat bones will be at different angles, his weight unevenly distributed and his horse's movements will be affected. A little slip such as this must be picked up immediately and corrected, so riders need somebody on the ground to ensure that they and the horse are not making unnecessary errors. It helps, too, to have someone else urging them to do everything just a little bit better, to try just that little bit harder, and this is why dressage riders subject themselves to the continuous critical but positive help of an assistant.

For some, the assistant is a wife, sister or parent; for others, it might be a fellow competitor; but for the majority of top Continental riders it is a professional trainer. The great combination of Christine Stückelberger and Granat relies on the ex-chief rider from the Spanish Riding School, Georg Vahl. The petite Swiss girl and the huge Holstein horse spent long sessions in the practice arena at Goodwood, but never without Vahl's sharp eye resting on them. Theirs has been a great rider/trainer relationship, and the assistance of this brilliant trainer helps to explain how such a waif of a girl can manage the wayward Granat.

Many riders are more independent. They might work a good deal at home on their own but pay regular visits to their trainer and make sure he is with them to help with riding-in at such major occasions as the Festival.

The Rumanian Georg Theodorescu, who defected to live in Germany, is a trainer with many such pupils. At the Festival he had a busy time helping his trainees, who had come from countries as far afield as Canada and Japan.

The one vital factor, whether the ground assistant is a professional trainer or another competitor, is that there is a rapport. For this, the rider and trainer should know each other well. The rider must respect his assistant's view. His assistant must know what advice can be acted on to improve, not spoil, the performance in that short space of time before horse and rider enter the arena.

Just before entering the test arena the riding-in – whether it was for three hours or less than an hour – should have resulted in the horse being not merely supple and obedient but eager to go forward, sensitive to the slightest command and bounding with power – which will make the extensions easy and the piaffe and passage spectacular and lively.

It is a dangerous and exciting position but to do well the rider must risk all: a calm performance which is obedient but lifeless, and therefore lacking in expression, earns few marks. The good dressage rider is brave enough to create power during his riding-in and then skilful enough to control it.

Right A final polish for the riding boots.

Below The riding-in is over and the bandages (used for protection) have to be removed before the test. Uwe Schulten-Baumer looks on while the final preparations are made.

Above Patricia Gardiner and Manifesto from Great Britain are here seen ready for the test and have just left the practice arena to go down to the international arena.

THE COMPETITION

The ultimate competition for all dressage riders is the Olympic Games. It attracts the best contestants from all over the world, as do the World Championships, which, like the Games, are held every four years, but two years after the Olympics.

The Continental Championships are confined to riders from that continent, i.e. Europe or America. These are held every two years, in the years between the Olympics and World Championships. Annually there are the Official International Shows (abbreviated to CDIOs), the most popular and competitive of which are held at Aachen (Germany) and Rotterdam (Holland).

CDIOs, World and Continental Championships run both individual and team competitions which are confined to amateur riders. The only international honours the professionals can compete for are at the smaller international shows known as CDIs and CDAs. At these events there are no official team competitions.

All these international events are controlled by the equestrian world's ruling body, the Fédération Equestre Internationale (FEI). It is this organization which lays down the rules, devises the tests and appoints the judges for international dressage competitions.

Competitiveness

The results of dressage competitions are decided by human judgement. This means they are not as clear-cut or easily understandable as in other eques-

trian sports, in which clearing jumps or speed determines the winner. The dressage judges analyse the performance and mark accordingly. The basic standards which determine these marks are discussed, and illustrated, in the pages that follow.

The dressage competition does lack, for most spectators, the competitiveness of other sports. This is because the sport retains the traditions developed when dressage was a form of display and not a competition. The authorities have taken care (to quote from the FEI rule book) 'to preserve the Equestrian Art from the abuses to which it can be exposed and to preserve it in the purity of its principles so that it can be handed on intact to generations of riders to come'. Dressage is therefore characterized by the upholding of purist standards (an increasingly rare feature in today's sports); accordingly, it avoids the excessive competitiveness, commercialization and the 'jazzier' approach of certain other sports.

For the participants the competition is a battle with the test. Each movement is a challenge, for it has to be performed better than ever before. But for the spectator, dressage remains a crossbreed – partly display, partly competition – and to get more than the aesthetic enjoyment of watching the obvious fluency, control and power of the great combinations, it is vital to achieve an understanding of those principles the FEI are preserving. Once a connoisseur of dressage, many fascinating hours can be spent watching. It is hoped that the following chapters will help towards this end.

THE CHAMPIONS

The colour section demonstrates the expertise of the riders and horses who won the highest places in the individual championship, the Grand Prix Special.

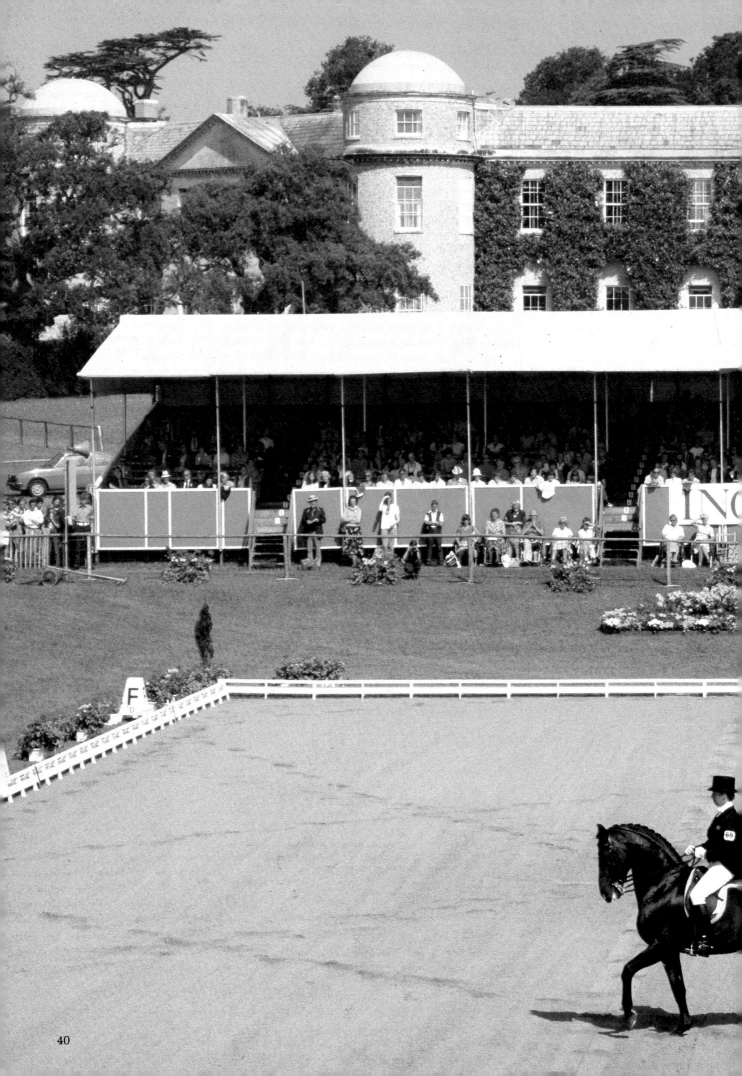

THE TEST

The dressage test, as its name implies, tests the horse and rider, mainly in their training, ability and arena craft. It consists of a series of movements which at international level are always performed from memory in an arena 60 × 20 metres.

There are four international standards, the aim of which is to provide progressive tests so that the horse is gradually brought to the highest level of competitive training: the Grand Prix. The easiest international test is the Prix St Georges, which is suitable for horses a little over halfway through their training. The next two tests, the Intermédiaires I and II, are intermediate tests that lead towards the ultimate test, the Grand Prix. The Grand Prix includes all the fundamental movements of the Classical High School. It does not include the paces based on extreme extension of the forelegs (e.g. the Spanish Walk), or the school leaps (e.g. Levade). These paces are obsolete in most schools other than the Spanish Riding School, Saumur and some Portuguese stables. The Grand Prix test decides the major team competition at all Olympic, World and Continental Championships and CDIOs. In these competitions each country is represented by its three best riders, whose scores, added together, provide a total.

Although there is always an individual winner in the Grand Prix, the most prestigious individual honours are earned in the Grand Prix Special. Only the top twelve combinations in the Grand Prix qualify for this test. Although this contains the same artistic equitation as the Grand Prix, it is shorter, the work is more concentrated, and the movements are demanded in more difficult areas of the arena. As only the best qualify, this test has become known as the Ride-off, and is undoubtedly the most exciting part of any dressage show. With the shorter test and fewer competitors it is easier, even for the layman, to compare and therefore judge performances. Consequently, as so many movements are condensed into the test, which contains frequent and extreme changes of pace, the display – as well as the competitive aspect – is more dramatic.

The Free Style

The Grand Prix Special might be the most exciting form of dressage competition, but the most aesthetic is the Free Style, or KUR, in which competitors revert to more traditional forms of dressage and perform the classical airs where, how and when they like. For this, although the conditions in the schedule stipulate which movements have to be performed and state a time-limit for the performance, the competitor can create a programme which suits his horse and is pleasing to the eye. Instead of the horse being asked to do movements in difficult and exact places the rider can select the moments which suit his horse. Thus in a Free Style competition, with its freedom of choice, we see the artistic and creative element emerging. This is further emphasized if the competitors are allowed music. Those with flair can choose music to suit the rhythm of the movements, the paces and the way their horse moves. Musical interpretation has become a feature of ice skating and, as an easily appreciated and pleasing approach, is a major reason for the sport's growing popularity. In dressage there have been relatively few musical

The test arena.

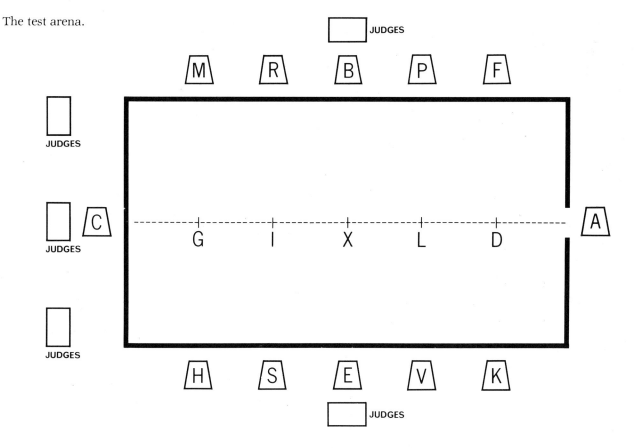

Free Styles, and competitors have had little opportunity and incentive to develop this crowd-pleasing aspect. The emphasis in dressage competitions has been on the technical; and the results are as far as possible decided according to specified standards.

When considering a painting or a piece of music there can be no absolute standards. Likewise, in dressage, as soon as artistic merits (musical interpretation, programme etc.) are judged then the personal likes and dislikes of a judge must play a part. The musical Free Style may be more fun for competitor and spectators, more comprehensible and more beautiful, but it may not be the fairest way of finding the most talented horse-and-rider combination. Ice-skating's answer has been to combine the results of the compulsory figures (which attract few spectators) and the free style to find the overall winner. In the future this might be done in dressage. At present, the free style is an isolated class which many pundits consider a frivolous bit of fun.

The marks

A dressage test is devised so as to make it as easy as possible to judge fairly. In the international tests there are between thirty and forty different movements to be marked. After a competitor has completed one of these movements, most judges remark to themselves one of ten reactions such as 'excellent', 'good' or 'bad'. For each of these reactions there is an appropriate mark: if the movement was 'excellent' (very rare) the mark is 10; 'very good' = 9; 'good' = 8; 'fairly good' = 7; 'satisfactory' = 6; 'sufficient' = 5; 'insufficient' = 4; 'fairly bad' = 3; 'bad' = 2; 'very bad' = 1; 'not executed' = 0.

Coefficients and weighting

Some movements are considered more important than others. In the Grand Prix, for example, each of the two canter pirouettes has a coefficient of 2, so that 40 (as opposed to 20) of the 420 marks in the test are allotted to the canter pirouettes. Also, the work in the piaffe and passage, the most difficult competitive dressage movements, is divided into twelve short sections so that 120 marks are given for these, that is, 35 per cent of the total marks.

An error in the changes will be obvious to the crowd, and many will wonder why a competitor who makes such an error could still win, but a set of

Above This horse is on the bit, and apart from showing a hint of tension conforms to the Fédération Equestre Internationale's definition of this prerequisite of good dressage.

Above This horse is slightly above the bit, but he does not appear to be resisting so badly as to open his mouth or pull against the rider's hand. It is probably only a momentary problem. He is said to be in front of the vertical (i.e. his nose is forward of the perpendicular line from his forelock).

Above This horse has come behind the bit. Despite the light rein contact he is holding his head down. This may be due to a number of factors such as loss of balance or simply evasion of the aids. He is said to be 'behind the vertical' for his nose is behind that perpendicular line from his ears.

changes is only one movement and the competitor will probably have lost only 3 or 4 marks for such an error.

If he fails, however, to establish a good passage or to move smoothly into the piaffe, he will lose many marks because this embodies a host of movements. It is this weighting of the movements, the heavy emphasis on certain aspects, which makes the dressage test a rigorous judgement of ability, but does *not* make it easy for onlookers to assess total marks.

Collective marks

Spectators tend to base their judgements on general impression – on how pleasing the performance as a whole was to the eye. The judges also take this into consideration when awarding what are known as the collective marks for paces, impulsion, submission and the rider's position. In the Grand Prix these collective marks are awarded 80 points, which account for 16 per cent of the total.

The marks for general impression do reflect the standard of performance in the movements, for unless the horse has good paces, impulsion, is submissive and the rider sits in a good position, the movements cannot be done well. Paces, impulsion, submission and good riding are the basics of dressage. Anybody who can assess how far a competitor has achieved them in a test will have a pretty good idea of the judges' placing of competitors.

The paces

Paces are the basics upon which the rider has least influence. Exceptional paces (together with good temperament and a sound conformation) are what riders seek in a potential dressage horse: they provide the natural talent. A dressage horse should have athletic paces, be light and nimble on his feet and have the scope to take short, springy strides or free, long-swinging ones.

It is the freedom of paces that the judges value. Of particular importance is the ability to take long, swinging strides in the extended walk, with the hindfoot coming well forward of the imprint of the corresponding forefoot. In the trot, the steps should be light and elastic and the strides should be long in the extension. In the canter the horse should be light on his feet and each stride should have spring.

Other features of the paces which the judges observe are the rhythm of the hoofbeats (the paces should be regular) and the sequence of the footfalls. These are what poor training can destroy. The walk is a marching pace of four-time with equal intervals between each hoofbeat. This is a pace that is often spoiled by poor training, in which case the hoofbeats become uneven. Sometimes only two hoofbeats can be heard, which means that both feet on one side are swinging forward together (this is known as an amble).

At the trot, the rhythm is two-time with a moment

Above This appears to be a good walk, the horse showing the ability to take long, sweeping strides.

Above This horse is showing that he has sufficient balance in his trot to take long, free strides.

Above A canter showing great energy and spring – something dressage riders appreciate.

of suspension when all four feet are off the ground. In a poor trot there is no moment of suspension (and therefore no spring), but the other extreme – too long a suspension – is bad too, for it may turn into the passage.

At the canter, three hoofbeats should be heard, followed by a moment of suspension. However, if the canter lacks bounce and activity it often deteriorates into four-time.

Impulsion

The second collective mark is for impulsion. This is the horse's power, or store of energy. If he has plenty of it, he can go forward whenever asked, extend as much as his ability allows and put elevation into his strides. It is an equally important factor for show-jumpers, who need to build up impulsion in order to have the power to spring over the fences.

A horse which has little or no impulsion might perform a test obediently, but he will appear lazy, lack vitality and spirit and show little variation of pace. It is impulsion which gives dressage its excitement, for handling a horse with great impulsion means controlling a very powerful, sensitive mechanism. Sometimes riders are unable to do so and the horse will explode into bucks or gallop across the arena.

Horses born with an ability and desire to go forward have the basis of impulsion, but in the main it is created by the rider. By using his driving aids (the seat and the legs) the rider encourages his horse to use his hindquarters more actively, to put his hindlegs further under the body and to take higher steps with his hindlegs. This movement of the hindquarters creates power in a similar manner to the compression of a spring. However, the hindquarters are only one end of the spring, and if only the driving aids are applied the horse will simply go faster. The

Above Here, the hindquarters of Ultimo are not engaged so his hindlegs are not coming far enough under his body. In this outline it will be difficult for his rider to generate sufficient impulsion.

Above In this movement Ultimo has his hindquarters distinctly engaged. The back, just behind the saddle, is rounded as opposed to hollow (or dipped) (see photograph opposite). The hindquarters have been lowered with the hindlegs coming well under the body, as opposed to them trailing behind (again, see photograph opposite).

rider's hands restrain with the reins so that the forward momentum is contained, and the horse becomes more or less (according to whether he is collected or extended) compressed like a spring. To achieve the full effect of the compression it is vital that the horse's body is supple enough to be compressed, and that the muscles of the neck and back – the connecting link between the hindquarters and the mouth – all operate freely. Any resistance, stiffness or crookedness of the body will restrict the connection between the hindquarters and the mouth, thereby hindering co-ordinating actions and the compression. Therefore horses with stiff backs, or with bodies which are bent when moving along straight lines, cannot contain so much energy (impulsion).

A horse which has impulsion is supple, straight, takes springy, elastic steps at the trot and canter, and is capable of spectacular extensions – for the release of a little of the power enables him to lengthen his strides.

Submission

Impulsion gives a horse power, but this must be controllable – and controllability, or submission, is the consideration of the third collective mark. Harmony between horse and rider is the vital aspect of this mark, for submission does not call for the horse's dour subservience, simply his willingness and ability to do the required work. The horse should accept the aids of the rider without resistance, and remain 'on the bit'. When 'on the bit' the head is steady, with the nose on or slightly in front of a vertical line running from his forelock to the ground (see photograph p. 50). The poll, not the crest of the neck or the withers, should be the highest point. The horse should accept a light, soft contact with the rider through the reins and not show any signs of resistance such as opening the mouth, putting out the tongue, grinding the teeth or swishing the tail. He should be happy in his work.

Submission entails not just the willingness but also the ability to do the work. To achieve this the horse must be manoeuvrable, and this is only possible if he is not on his forehand. That is, the hindquarters should carry the majority of his and the rider's weight. This is achieved by engagement of the hindquarters, so that the hindlegs step further under the body and are therefore able to carry more of the weight and not to push it. With the weight lightened off the forehand they will become more mobile, manoeuvrable and light. The horse will find it easier to go sideways, to extend or collect, and he will be more pleasurable to ride and to watch.

Rider's position

Finally, a collective mark is given for the rider. This accounts for only 20 marks, just 4 per cent of the total in the Grand Prix. This gives riders little incentive to apply only subtle, imperceptive aids. In their quest to perfect movements and to generate impulsion riders can become over-zealous, applying obvious aids and creating a less aesthetic impression for spectators. This will have little effect on the judges' marking for as long as riders persuade their horses to work well they will only lose 2 or 3 marks. The judges concentrate on the horses, not the riders.

The standards for the rider, as laid down by the FEI, are high. He is supposed to ride without apparent effort, maintaining his balance, with his upper body easy, free and erect, his loins and hips supple, and his thighs and legs steady and well stretched down. The hands should be low and close together with the thumbs uppermost. The elbows should be close to the body. In this position the rider should be able to follow the movements of the horse smoothly and freely and to apply his aids imperceptibly.

If the general impression of a test is good and the collective marks are high, it means that the horse is athletic and talented (paces), energetic and supple (impulsion), obedient and manoeuvrable (submission), and that the rider is able to maintain a classical position and use discreet aids (position).

Above Uwe Sauer from Germany has one of the best positions on a horse and is able to maintain it throughout the test. Some might, however, criticize him for bringing his body behind the vertical when using his driving aids.

Above The French school of Saumur is renowned for producing riders who sit in a good position. One of their members, M. Flament, is an excellent representative. The half pass shown here is a particularly difficult movement for the rider to remain, as required, in alignment with the horse.

The results of dressage competitions are determined by judges. In international competitions there are five, which may seem a high number but helps to ensure the fairest possible result.

Value of different opinions

The judges are not robots; human judgements are involved in their decisions and therefore differences of opinion are bound to emerge. Say, for example, that a horse produces a magnificent extended trot but loses his balance and breaks into the canter for a stride. A judge who values accuracy highly will give him a low mark, whereas another judge who values impulsion and talent highly might only deduct 1 or 2 points. Such differences of opinion do have benefits and should not be criticized out of hand.

Dressage, as an artistic sport, does have a variety of schools and approaches. If judges had absolute standards to which they had to adhere, only one school would be possible and the artistic and individual element might well be stifled. The present system provides the opportunity for different styles and types of horses to be appreciated, even if not by all judges. There will be occasions when a competitor feels he has been harshly marked, but these are usually balanced by the occasions when he has been generously marked. The usual benefit of having five judges in international competitions is that a balance is achieved amongst them.

Differences in the marking between judges might be the cause of criticism and some bewilderment to competitors, but the variation allows for artistic licence. It ensures that various styles, as long as they are based on the classic principles, have the opportunity to be appreciated by the judges.

Justifiable variations in marks

On many occasions there will be great differences in the marks given by the various judges. This should not affect results as long as the placings are the same. One judge may be marking generously, giving 8s and 9s for the best performers, whereas another may have higher standards and only give a mere 5 or 6 for equivalent movements. The final scores of these judges may be 100 marks apart, but it is of no consequence if they have placed the same horses 1st, 2nd and 3rd. To express horror at the differences between the judges' scores is only justifiable if they have placed different competitors in the first three places.

Every sport, none the less, has its moments of unfairness. A show-jumper might just brush a fence and it will come down, but on another occasion he

		TEST	DIRECTIVE IDEAS	Marks	Points	Correction	Coefficient	Total
1	A X	Enter at collected canter Halt - Immobility - Salute Proceed at collected trot	The entry. The halt and the transitions to and from the halt.	10				
2	C HXF F	Track to the left Change rein at extended trot Collected trot	The extension and regularity of the steps. The transitions.	10				
3	VXR	Half-pass	The correctness and the regularity. The carriage and the bend. The balance.	10				
4	CHS SEV VKA A	Extended trot Collected trot Extended trot Collected trot	The extension and regularity of the steps - even through the corners. The collection The transitions The balance.	10				
5	PXS	Half-pass	The correctness and the regularity. The carriage and the bend. The balance.	10				
6	CMR RBP PFA A	Extended trot Collected trot Extended trot Collected trot	The extension and regularity of the steps - even through the corners. The collection. The transitions. The balance.	10				
7	KLBIH H	Extended walk Collected walk	The extension and regularity of the steps. The transitions.	10			2	
8	HCMG	Collected walk	The shortening and heightening of the steps. The carriage and the regularity.	10				
9	G	Piaffer 10 to 12 steps	The cadence and regularity.	10				
10	G	Proceed at passage. The transitions from the collected walk to the piaffer and from the piaffer to the passage		10				
11	GHSI RBX	Passage	The cadence and regularity.	10				
12	X	Piaffer 10 to 12 steps	The cadence and regularity.	10				
13	X	Proceed at passage. The transitions from the passage to the piaffer and from the piaffer to the passage		10				
14	XEVL PFA	Passage	The cadence and regularity.	10				
15	A KXM M	Extended trot. Change rein at extended trot Collected trot	The extension and regularity of the steps - even through the corner. The transitions.	10				
16	C SXP P	Collected canter Half-pass Change of leg	The correctness and the regularity. The carriage and the bend. The balance and the change of leg.	10				
			Forward	170				

		TEST	IDEES DIRECTRICES	Marks	Points	Correction	Coefficient	Total
			Carried forward	170				
17	VXR R	Half-pass Change of leg	The correctness and the regularity. The carriage and the bend The balance and the change of leg.	10				
18	HXF	On the diagonal, 9 changes of leg every 2nd stride, (finishing on the right leg)	The correctness, straightness, balance and fluency.	10				
19	KXM	On the diagonal, 15 changes of leg every stride, (finishing on the left leg)	The correctness, straightness, balance and fluency.	10				
20	HK K	Extended canter Collected canter	The extension. The straightness. The transitions.	10				
21	A D	Down centre line Pirouette to the left	The collection. The regularity.	10			2	
22	Between D and G	On the centre line 9 changes of leg every stride (finishing on the right leg)	The correctness, straightness, balance and fluency.	10				
23	G C	Pirouette to the right. Track to the right.	The collection. The regularity.	10			2	
24	MF F	Extended canter Collected canter	The extension. The straightness. The transitions.	10				
25	A D	Down centre line and, immediately after the turn, collected trot Passage	The turn, and the transitions from collected canter to collected trot and from collected trot to passage.	10				
26	DI	Passage	The cadence and regularity.	10				
27	I	Piaffer 10 to 12 steps	The cadence and regularity.	10				
28	I	The transition from the passage to the piaffer.		10				
29	I	After the piaffer - Halt - Immobility - Salute	The halt and the transition.	10				
		Leave arena at a walk on a long rein at A	Total	320				
		Collective marks						
		1. Paces (freedom and regularity)		10			2	
		2. Impulsion (desire to move forward, elasticity of the steps, suppleness of the back and engagement of the hind quarters)		10			2	
		3. Submission (attention and confidence; harmony, lightness and ease of the movements; acceptance of the bridle and lightness of the forehand)		10			2	
		4. Rider's position and seat; correctness and effect of the aids		10			2	
		To be deducted	Total	400				

— For every commenced second exceeding the time allowed : 1/2 mark
— Errors of the course and omissions are penalised

1st time = 2 marks
2nd time = 4 marks
3rd time = 8 marks
4th time = Elimination

| | | | Total | | |

Above Grand Prix Special test sheet.

Above Three of the judges' boxes are on the short side of the arena at the opposite end to the entry (at A). The President, with his writer and timekeeper, is always in the centre box. Horses often spook at the boxes and Dr Reiner Klimke is seen here familiarizing his horse with them.

Above The two remaining boxes are in the middle of the long sides at B and on the opposite side at E. Mrs Hansen (far right) is seen here judging Gabriela Grillo on Ultimo.

might hit it so hard that the elements rock back and forth, yet it does not fall. The real difference is that the show-jumper can only call such occurrences bad luck, whereas dressage riders can blame the judges.

Positions

The dressage judges are placed around the arena so that they can inspect the performance from as many angles as possible. This is important, for the standard of a movement may vary when viewed from different positions. The straightness of the horse, for example, can be readily evaluated if viewed head on or from behind, but is very difficult to ascertain from the side. Movements give different impressions when viewed from different angles, which is yet another reason for variations in the judges' marks.

The FEI has laid down the positions which, in their view, give the fairest viewing. The President sits at

Above Ulrich Lehmann and Widin in the test arena. **Below** The test is over for Anne-Marie Sanders-Keyzer and Amon; but for the judges there are still a few important marks to be given. These are the collective marks for paces, impulsion, submission and rider's position.

Above The judges' day may last from 8 a.m. to 6 p.m. In this picture the international judges Mrs Gold and Mrs Jook Hall from Great Britain, Mrs Hansen from Denmark, and Colonel Thackeray from the USA are seen during a break walking back to their refreshment tent with their writers.

the end of the centre line with one judge on either side (7.50 metres away). Two further judges sit in the middle of the long sides (at B and E).

Test sheets

Every judge has a writer who records on the test sheet (a separate one for each horse) the mark the judge has awarded for each movement. The judge will often make remarks, giving reasons for a high or low mark, which the writer records in a separate column. The test sheets are collected, the totals added up by scorers and the results announced to the general public. The collection of the test sheets and addition of the marks means there is an inevitable delay between the performance and the results.

Other systems of announcing results

In some of the less purist dressage events, these delays which, after all, reduce the impact of a result and the competitiveness of the event – are avoided. In some Free Styles (at which it is usual for just three judges to preside), judges hold up their scores at the end of the test in a similar manner to the scoring of ice skating. Their marks are confined to two categories: one for artistic impression, one for technical merit. This simpler system with its quicker results is appreciated by spectators.

The most direct system is used at Badminton Horse Trials. When a judge awards a mark for a movement, he presses the appropriate button and the mark is flashed up on a scoreboard. This system is much more exciting – and instructive – for the crowd, enabling laymen to find out what is good and

bad and make their own evaluations accordingly.

Such crowd-pleasing scoring systems are not allowed at international championships, in which the purist aspects are preserved and promoted. This does make the judge's task a little easier, for he has time to reflect and to adjust marks when he is not being pressurized into an immediate assessment.

Qualities of judges

The judge's task is hard. He must be able to bear that dire responsibility of deciding who is the best; all the competitors rely on him to reach a fair decision. There are, too, the pressures of fearing that his evaluation may not be in line with that of the other judges, which could leave him open to severe criticism; moreover, a moment's slip in his concentration could result in his missing a major occurrence.

The judge must have the ability to make a quick evaluation, to have a perceptive eye, enabling him to see all the important good and bad points in a movement. He must not over-react to one petty mistake. He must be able to maintain the same standard of marking from the first to the last horse; these might perform at anything up to eight hours apart.

The judge's work is hard and responsible. Although his decisions are based on the standards discussed in the following pages these cannot be absolute. It would make his job much easier if they could be, but his personal tastes must play a small part as long as the artistic element is retained. The alternative would be for dressage to turn into more of a technical craft, in which accuracy is the most important factor. This trend already exists, but it is not one that most people wish to see pursued.

THE ENTRY

The steward's inspection

Five or ten minutes before a competitor is due in the arena the steward carries out an inspection. He has to see that all obligatory pieces are worn (spurs, double bridle, saddle), that they are of a permissible type (the bit must be a double and may only be one of eight specified variations) and that prohibited items are not worn (brushing boots have to be removed, and no gadgetry or mechanisms for forcing the horse to obey are allowed).

Most riders use this inspection time to spruce themselves up, and to try to make their general turn-out immaculate and attractive. Not many minutes can be spent on these final preparations, for the horse needs to be kept warm, active and supple.

Immediately before the 'test', most riders ask their horses for short stretches of collected work alternated with opportunities to relax, for the horse needs to catch his breath before the trial ahead. This ensures control of a calm but energetic horse.

Familiarization

When the previous competitor leaves the arena on a long rein it is time for the next competitor to walk down towards the sand arena. All too often the horse tenses up at the sight of the stands full of people, the flowers, the flags and the gaily decorated little judges' boxes around the arena; it all appears quite startling after the unadorned practice arena. The rider has just a few minutes to familiarize his horse with the scene and to rid him of any tension which will destroy suppleness. Most remedy this with quick series of extensions and collections which demand the horse's attention, stimulate suppleness and help to rid him of any mischievous spirits.

Entering

When the bell goes the horse and rider are on parade, and should canter round to where the attendant holds open the barrier (at A). They must now enter the arena – an empty, sand-covered area, ready for them alone, surrounded by a host of inquisitive eyes. The judges and spectators will be quicker to criticize than to praise – but they must ride bravely, and even risk making mistakes. If they ride cautiously, simply trying to avoid errors, the prizes will not be theirs. As they canter on to the sand, they must be daring and ride positively to produce their best.

This is when that vital concentration counts. The surroundings must be obliterated from the mind; the only thing that matters is to collect the horse into a very controlled canter and to go straight down the centre line. The hindquarters must not swing to left or right, nor must they go too fast, for then it is difficult to come to a smooth halt at X. The horse, although keen to go forward, must not pull, the rein contact must be soft and the horse's forehand light, otherwise he will find it difficult to engage the hindquarters in the manner that the sharp halt from the canter demands.

The half halt

Most riders use the half halt to keep their horses light and collected down the centre line (that is, they only half ask for a halt). They apply the aids for the halt, but only momentarily, relaxing them before the horse has time to halt. They apply the seat and legs to make the hindquarters, the source of power, more active, and then momentarily restrain with the hands. The result should be a barely perceptible compression, a slight lowering of the hindquarters

Above Dr Reiner Klimke and Ahlerich from Germany are soon to enter the arena. This experienced rider is spending the last few valuable minutes before the judge's bell is rung familiarizing his young horse with the atmosphere of the competition.

Above Whips may not be carried in international-class tests. Most riders like to take them down to the arena to encourage a horse which spooks at the strange sights. Gabriela Grillo from Germany is seen here handing her whip over to the steward before starting her test.

Above Diana Mason, Britain's Chairman of Dressage, and Special Edition, take their first steps on to the arena. The horse appears a little heavy in the hand and his rider is working hard to correct this using her legs and seat to ask him to engage his hindquarters.

Above Ulrich Lehmann is about to enter the arena. From this moment every step, every action is vital; it is now that the relatively small area of sand looks huge, lonely and foreboding, for within its confines the competitor will prove whether he is good, bad, indifferent or (very occasionally) outstanding.

Above Ulrich Lehmann has applied a strong half-halt to help collect the canter prior to the halt on the centre line. The effects are easily seen with the hindquarters becoming more engaged: the hindquarters slightly lowered, the head and neck rising, and the whole horse's outline rounding up.

and a warning that something is about to happen. Good riders use these half halts all the time, to encourage the horse to be more active, to make him attentive and to warn him of impending action.

The halt

As the horse approaches X the canter is made slower. The more advanced the horse, the slower the speed that is possible, but he cannot be slowed down so much that he resists by swinging his hindquarters to one side, or evades the rein contact, or loses the three-time beat of the canter.

He should be brought to a smooth, almost instantaneous, halt standing straight along the centre line. He should be four square: that is, with the front legs side by side and the hindlegs also in a pair. A square halt is one of the judges' specific requirements, for it proves that the horse is balanced, with his weight evenly distributed; any deviation loses marks.

The move off

The horse should remain at X, motionless, while the rider takes the reins in one hand and salutes the judges. He should be willing to move forward instantaneously into the trot, without swerving to either side or coming behind or above the bit, as soon as the rider has collected his reins and applied the aids.

First impressions

The major consideration for the judges when they evaluate the entry is that the horse is straight, that the transitions into and from the halt are smooth and that the halt is square. It is, however, the moment in which those vital first impressions are formed. Competitors who appear confident in their talent and harmonious in their partnership create a good first impression, and this tends to be reflected by the judges in their marking.

Features	
Good	**Bad**
On the bit	Above/behind the bit
Calm, submissive	Resisting, tilting head
Collected	On forehand
Straight	Crooked, wavering
Transitions fluent and instantaneous	Abrupt, rough transitions; too long taken to establish
Halt square	Fore- and/or hindlegs not in pairs (oblique halt)
Halt motionless	Moved forward, backwards or sideways

A

B

C

D

E

F

Above Rinie Schaft from Holland on Monseigneur canters in to halt and salute. In **A** the horse is in a pleasing collected canter in a good outline with the hindquarters well engaged, and the rider is relaxed. In **B** they are about to reach X and the rider has applied his seat, leg and rein aids. The effects in **C** are dramatic with the hindlegs coming well under the body but sadly he must have become a little unbalanced for in **D** the rider is having to apply his reins quite strongly and the hindquarters have not remained as far under the body as is needed for high marks. Also in **E** the left hindleg is behind the right and the head has dropped a little from its original good height. In the move off the loss of balance and engagement has resulted in his being a little on his forehand.

THE FIGURES

A number of figures (circles, voltes, serpentines and figures of eight) are used in dressage tests. They all involve turning and some changes of direction.

Turns

When a horse turns he should maintain the rhythm of the pace, take strides of an even size and keep his body on the arc of the turn. To remain on the arc, the hindlegs must follow in the same tracks as the forelegs, so he needs to be bent slightly throughout his whole body. If the horse remains straight during a turn, the hindquarters tend to swing to the outside as the forehand is directed around. On the other hand, if he is too bent, he curls to the inside and his hindlegs step to the inside of the tracks of the forelegs. The horse's head should be turned just far enough for the rider to see his inside eye. With this slight bend the horse should be able to keep his fore- and hindlegs on the same track. Then it will be easier for him to take even strides, to remain balanced and to keep up the same rhythm through the turn as on straight lines. However, the smaller the radius of the turn, the more the horse will have to be bent throughout the length of his body.

Voltes

The tiniest circle a horse is asked to complete on one track is known as a volte (the pirouette is smaller but here the forelegs move laterally). The volte is a circle of 6 metres' diameter. A horse can only do this at the collected (and working) paces. It is also the approximate diameter of the part of a circle which a trained horse should make when turning a corner. Therefore a horse in the collected paces should complete a quarter of a volte through each turn in the arena. At the medium and extended paces this can be enlarged to part of the arc of a 10-metre-diameter circle.

Figures of eight

The figure of eight consists of two voltes (in international tests) or two circles (in less difficult tests). The voltes, or circles, should be of equal size and joined at the centre. On completion of the first volte or circle, the aim should be to make the horse straight for just an instant before establishing the opposite bend and starting the second volte or circle.

Serpentines

The serpentine consists of a series of loops running from one long side of the arena to the other, and the horse is asked for a change of bend and direction as he crosses the centre line. In international tests the serpentine is used for canter work, and some of the loops are made in counter canter. In the easiest test (Prix St Georges) just four loops are performed, so their diameter is relatively large, at least in comparison to those in Intermédiaire II, in which six loops are required.

Above Ulrich Lehmann shows great rapport with his horse. The horse has the collection to go deeply into the corner and the centrifugal force created by so doing is shown by how far he and his rider have tipped from the normal right-angle to the ground. To remain in balance the rider must follow the same angle and not slip to the outside.

The most important requirements for a serpentine are that the loops are of an even size; that the change of bend is distinctly shown when the new direction is asked for on the centre line; and that the first loop is started after the middle of the short side with the horse gradually moving away, and therefore not going into the second corner. Similarly the serpentine ends with the horse coming back to the track in the middle of the short side, and again he should not go into the first corner prior to doing this.

Features	
Good	**Bad**
On the bit	Above/behind the bit
Rein contact light but positive	Tilting head
Strides remain even	Strides shorten or lengthen
Correct bend distinctly shown	Straight, or wrong bend
Supple	Stiff
Balance and rhythm maintained through turns	Rhythm changed, runs or slows up
Accurate figures	Inaccurate figures

A

B

Above Cindy Neale from Canada on Equus seen in a right volte (6-metre circle) **A** and in a left volte **B**. Equus appears to be bent the same amount to the right in **A** as he is to the left in **B**. He seems well-balanced and is not tilting his head (one of the commonest evasions when turning in a tight circle). In both circles the rider is giving the horse great support with her inside leg, which helps the horse to bend his body around it.

THE COLLECTED WALK

Riding forward to collection

In the collected walk the horse should take short, active steps. This shortening of the strides is not achieved by resisting with the reins to slow the walk down: such a method results in the hindlegs falling behind rather than stepping well under the body, the steps becoming less active with the limbs being dragged rather than flexed; the power will have been lost. Instead, the horse is ridden forward into the collected walk. The rider applies the driving aids of the seat and legs to ask the horse to use his hindlegs more actively, to place them further under his body and thus slightly lower his hindquarters. At the same time the rider restrains but does not pull with the reins. The result of these actions should be shorter, higher steps, with each hindfoot placed on the ground just behind the corresponding forefoot; the neck raised and arched; the head close to the vertical (positioned on a vertical line from the ground) and a light contact through the reins to the rider's hands.

Thus the horse is collected into a short outline, with the steps becoming more elevated and the head and neck raised. The horse has been compressed, and so should the energy have been. It is not good collection if he has been pulled back into it with the reins rather than ridden up to it with the seat and legs.

Qualities of the walk

The walk must remain purposeful and true (see glossary). Thus those four hoofbeats must come at regular intervals, with no suspicion of an amble (in which the walk deteriorates into two-time). Nor should the steps become quick and tense; but all this is very hard to achieve. If the rider drives too hard the rhythm is lost, if he does not drive hard enough there is insufficient energy and elevation.

As in so much of dressage, the rider has to balance on a knife-edge, that is, achieving enough of one requirement without losing too much of another. The rider must be constantly alert, always tempering the severity of his aids, changing the demands so that he keeps the best possible mixture of ingredients (impulsion, submission, etc.). If the rider dreams, or relaxes because he thinks he has achieved the ideal, he will soon lose that good mixture.

Above Ulrich Lehmann and Widin create a good impression at the collected walk. The horse is accepting a pleasing contact through the reins. He seems relaxed and his poll is just about the highest point. The poll is supposed to be the highest point, but this is rarely achieved in practice.

Above Ulrich Lehmann does not appear to have achieved such a good collected walk with his young horse Wörder. Although the head and neck are well raised the steps seem rather long, the hindquarters have not been lowered and the hindlegs are not well engaged.

Features	
Good	**Bad**
On the bit	Above/behind the bit
Outline shortened	Outline still long
Head vertical	Behind or in front of the vertical
Neck raised	
Rein contact light, horse in self-carriage	Head and neck too horizontal
Strides elevated and short	Strong, pulling, or no contact
Hoofbeats regular four-time	Trudging, longish strides with little flexion of joints
Distinct steady rhythm	
Level, both hindlegs used equally and both forelegs	Amble/irregular hoofbeats
	Hurried steps
Strides purposeful and active	Unlevel – one hindleg more active than the other
	Slow and lazy

Above Lendon Gray from the USA has Beppo in a true walk. Each leg is at a different stage of movement, and the four hoofbeats should have equal time intervals between them. However, the degree of collection is insufficient with the horse's outline being rather long: the head and neck are not sufficiently raised and the steps, too, could be shorter.

Above Having completed a walk pirouette, Bonnie Bonnello and Satchmo appear to have lost their balance in the collected walk. The horse has stiffened; his head has come in front of the vertical and his hindquarters are not well engaged. The sequence of the footfalls will only just be four-time as it can be seen that the near foreleg and hindleg are almost in the same stage of elevation.

THE MEDIUM WALK

This is the easiest variation of the walk. It is one which even novice horses can achieve quite naturally as the horse takes neither very short nor very long strides. The horse moves more freely than in the collected walk and is less constrained. The strides are longer, the head slightly lower and the neck slightly less arched. The rider maintains a similar light contact through the reins as in collection.

Overtracking

As the steps are longer in the medium than in the collected walk the hindfeet should overtrack; that is, each hindfoot should come further forward than the front foot on the same side.

This ability to overtrack is probably the most important feature of a good walk. It is difficult to develop, so few riders would contemplate buying a horse which does not naturally overtrack.

Use in tests

The medium walk, being a relatively easy pace, earns few marks in an advanced test. It is only asked for over a short distance, the main purpose being for the competitor to prove that he can show three distinct walks – collected, medium and extended. The horse must be able to produce enough difference in the elevation and length of his stride at the walk for the judges to recognize the three versions.

Below & opposite This series of photographs of Lendon Gray on Beppo illustrates both the change in outline and length of steps from the medium walk to the collected walk. The transition should have been made at arena point A, but in this case it was a little late. The rider has perhaps asked for more collection than the horse was capable of giving at that moment; he might not have been in a good balance or he might have stiffened, forcing her to use the reins to shorten him rather than riding him up to collection. The result is that in **F** his head has come just behind the vertical and in **G** he has shown his displeasure by slightly dipping his back and coming a little above the bit. The sequence of footfalls at the walk can be followed in this series (see page 143).

A

B

C

D

Below right Uwe Sauer on Hirtentraum completing the short medium walk which comes between the extended and the collected walk. The judges want to see distinct differences between collected, medium and extended walk (mainly in the length of steps and outline). Hirtentraum seems to be taking steps of medium length, and his head and neck are not so high as in collection.

E

F

G

Features	
Good	**Bad**
On the bit	Above/behind the bit
Head just in front of vertical	Head still vertical or too far out
Neck slightly lower and less arched than in collection	Neck too high or too low
	Pulling/no contact
Rein contact light and constant	Amble/irregular hoofbeats
	Unlevel
Hoofbeats regular four-time	Hindfeet fall short of corresponding forefeet
Level, both hindlegs used equally and both forelegs	Restricted, flicky strides, slothful, dragging limbs
Overtracks	
Strides free, unconstrained and energetic	

THE EXTENDED WALK

In the extended walk the horse lengthens his strides to the maximum. He also lowers his neck and stretches out his head so that it is forward of the vertical, but the rein contact must not be lost. Each hindleg should easily overtrack the corresponding foreleg.

Hurrying

This is a difficult version of the walk for the rider to establish: he has to get the horse to lengthen but not speed up. If he pushes too hard for the extension, the horse will start to hurry, shorten his strides and probably lose the rhythm of the pace. Even worse, he might break into the trot.

The rider has to remain very relaxed, and ease into rather than demand the lengthening. Any tension is relayed quickly to the horse at this pace, when everything happens slowly. If he does become tense, the rhythm is hindered, and the suppleness which is essential to achieve lengthening is restricted. The aim is purposeful, long, unhurried strides.

Value

The extended walk is considered an important reflection of the methods of training. Although some horses, by nature, have a poor extended walk, and are unable to overtrack, many more have their walk spoilt by bad training. Tensions, resistances, forceful training, and/or excessive work at the walk when maintaining a strong rein contact, all spoil the regularity and freedom of this pace.

Consequently, in international tests the extended walk is asked for over a relatively long distance (usually across the diagonal), and a coefficient of 2 is put on the mark. (A horse which has a poor extended walk will be marked badly in this section and in the collective mark for paces.) Thus the extended walk has an influence on 40 of the marks.

Features	
Good	**Bad**
On the bit	Above/behind the bit
Head and neck lengthened and lowered	Neck remains high
Rein contact light and constant	Heavy contact or loss of contact
Shoulder movement free and easy	Restricted or flicky strides
Hindquarters engaged	Dragging hindquarters
Overtracking distinctly	Hindfeet falling short of forefeet imprints
Hindlegs used equally	Unlevel
Hoofbeats regular, good rhythm	Irregular/amble
Strides long and purposeful	Short, hurried strides, speeding up rather than extending

Above Ulrich Lehmann has not been able to maintain rein contact when asking his young horse Wörder to lengthen his outline and steps in the extended walk.

Above Ulrich Lehmann and Widin in extended walk. The strides appear to be long and the horse has lowered and stretched out his head whilst maintaining a good rein contact. The photograph does not show if overtracking (where the hindfoot comes further forward than the forefoot's hoofprint on the same side) has occurred.

Above The successful young Dutch combination Frances Verbeek-van Rooy and Ivar in the extended walk. The horse's attention seems to have wandered, and although his face is well in front of the vertical, his head is a little high, making his outline hollow. From this position it will be difficult for the horse to overtrack.

Above Although Jennie Loriston-Clarke and Dutch Courage seem to be calm and relaxed in the extended walk, to achieve the higher marks there should be a more positive rein contact and lengthening of the outline.

THE COLLECTED TROT

The trot is usually the prettiest of the horse's paces. When done well the horse springs lightly from one pair of diagonal legs (near fore and off hind and vice versa), to the other pair, with a distinct moment of suspension in between when all the feet are off the ground. There should be more elasticity and power to this pace than to the walk. A flat trot in which the steps lack elasticity and the moment of suspension is minimal, or even non-existent, is neither so pretty, nor a source of such manoeuvrability and power.

The supple back

For a horse to spring from diagonal to diagonal he swings his body slightly (the tail can be seen to move from side to side). He can only do this if the muscles (especially in the back) are supple, working freely and equally on both sides. Such a horse is said to be 'through' as he is using his muscles throughout his body, and none is resistant or stiff.

A horse which is stiff in the back cannot use his muscles freely, and simply swings his legs back and forth as if they are attached to a plank of wood. The muscles through the back remain rigid so that the hindquarters must operate independently of the forehand and there will be no muscle movement in the back co-ordinating the actions of the fore- and hindlegs.

In dressage, the outcome of this is that the horse will be unable to compress his body like a spring because of the rigid area in the middle (his back). Therefore the trot will lack impulsion (see glossary) and there will be little of the power and energy

Above John Winnett from the USA spends a good deal of time training in Europe. Although in this collected trot on Leopardi the horse's legs are pleasingly active, ideally the hindquarters could have been more engaged, with the hindlegs coming further under the body.

Above Reiner Klimke from Germany, who must have trained more Grand Prix horses than any other competitor, has Ahlerich in a pleasing collected trot. The horse is active and the outline is good.

Above Uwe Schulten Baumer and Slibovitz can produce a collected trot which is the equal of, or better than, any of their competitors. This huge chestnut Hanoverian can collect into a short outline fluently, and without stiffening. The result is a rhythmical and supple collected trot.

Above Rinie Schaft on Juroen from Holland. He has his horse taking short, active strides in a volte. To achieve these strides the pasterns have been pushed down to lie almost parallel to the ground.

Above Jennie Loriston-Clarke and Dutch Courage are renowned for their gay, fluent work. Their collected trot appears brisk and active; the horse's head and neck is well raised, and the rein contact pleasingly light.

Above This American combination is performing collected trot in the volte. It appears to be balanced, with the correct bend. Ideally the hindquarters could have been more engaged with the hindlegs coming further under the body.

needed for extensions, collection or lateral work. The rider might have a smooth ride but it will lack power, suppleness and excitement; he will not be maximizing the potential of his horse's physique. To the spectators it may look calm and even fluent, but it will lack expression, vitality and athleticism.

The swing of the trot is therefore indicative of suppleness and of the ability to build up impulsion. This impulsion is vital to achieve a good collected trot, and as in the walk, this impulsion is only retained and/or generated if the horse is ridden forward into collection rather than slowed down with the reins.

The collection

The results of riding the horse forward into collection at the trot are similar to those at the walk. The outline is shortened, the head raised and the steps made shorter and more elevated. The important difference is that the greater forwardness of the trot and the moment of suspension gives the horse more manoeuvrability. This reaches its maximum in collection when the extra engagement of the hindquarters and their slight lowering takes further the weight off the forehand to make it mobile.

Use of collected trot

This manoeuvrability at the collected trot means it is the version of the trot used for the most difficult movements. It is therefore used for the smallest circles (voltes) and for all the lateral work. The horse spends a great deal of the test in the collected trot although he is rarely going straight ahead.

Features	
Good	**Bad**
On the bit	Above/behind the bit
Outline shortened	Outline too horizontal
Head vertical	Behind or in front of the vertical
Head and neck raised	
Back supple with a slight swing to the movement	Head and neck too low
	Stiff in back
Strides short and elevated	Dragging limbs, little elasticity
Hoofbeats regular two-time	
	Irregular
Distinct moment of suspension	Flat trot
	Unlevel
Level, using both hindlegs equally, and both forelegs	Heavy
Light and mobile	

THE MEDIUM TROT

In the medium trot the strides are considerably longer than in collection, the head slightly lower and just in front of the vertical, the neck a tiny bit less arched.

Hurrying

The same features of the trot, such as a supple back and elasticity of steps, still hold. The essence of the medium trot is to establish a moderate extension of the strides without pushing so hard that the horse starts to hurry, speed up his rhythm, become tense and actually shorten his strides. It is the lengthening

of strides and outline which is required, not an increase of speed.

Even strides

The other major problem is to achieve a moderate extension at the required marker, and then to maintain this same length of stride until the movement ends. Few marks will be given if the strides are not even, with a pronounced and regular rhythm.

It is much more difficult to maintain a medium trot through corners and on circles, but this is what must be done in the international tests. To keep the

Above Anne-Grethe Jensen and Marzog from Denmark caught at a bad moment. Perhaps the horse tried to canter and the rider had to use her hands to stop him. The result is that the horse is heavy on the rein and behind the vertical. This has restricted the freedom of the horse's shoulder, the lightness of his forehand and his medium strides are flat and limited.

Above Christine Stückelberger on the American thoroughbred Turmalin. Her ability to ride this light, sensitive horse after the powerful Granat proves just how good a rider she is. In this medium trot there has been good, active lengthening of the strides, but the hindquarters are insufficiently engaged and the outline has become hollow.

Above Rinie Schaft on Juroen can be compared with the photograph on page 76 when in collected trot. This is a good, active medium trot, but the hindleg has not been lifted as high as the foreleg. The face being so far forward of the vertical suggests that the outline might be becoming a little hollow.

Above A pleasing, relaxed medium trot shown by Gabriela Grillo's very consistent horse, Ultimo. The strides are a good length and the outline distinctly longer than to be expected at the collected trot.

Above Lady Joicey and Sascha from Great Britain performing the medium trot on a circle. To keep the strides even, balanced and of a medium length while turning is a very difficult job for the rider. It also requires great suppleness and freedom on the part of the horse. This pair appear to be coping admirably.

Above Uwe Sauer and Hirtentraum in a medium trot on a circle. This strong, positive German rider helps his horse in this difficult movement. Note the use of the inside leg and the driving position of the seat.

Above To maintain the medium trot through the corners is difficult. Frances Verbeek-van Rooy appears to have her horse in good balance during this manoeuvre. The rein contact is light and the strides are still of medium length. The rider is assisting her horse well for she has remained over his centre of balance and is giving good support with her inside leg.

balance when taking long strides through a turn and to maintain the same length of stride and the same slow rhythm requires a talented rider and a very supple horse. All too few horses complete the 20-metre circles at the medium trot asked for in the Prix St Georges without losing their balance and starting to hurry.

It is better for the competitor to establish a less spectacular medium trot which can be maintained than to throw in a few excellent strides and lose the balance so that the horse starts to quicken and run.

Features	
Good	**Bad**
On the bit	Above/behind the bit
Head just in front of vertical	Head vertical or behind it
	Neck too high or low
Neck lower, less arched than in collection	Stiff in back
Back supple	Strides same size as in collection (too short) or extension (too long)
Strides of medium extension	
Strides even, free and unconstrained	Strides uneven, tense, restricted
Level strides	Unlevel strides

THE EXTENDED TROT

The extended trot can be one of the most spectacular dressage movements. The horse should be stretching his utmost for every stride, with the forelegs moving freely from the shoulders to reach way out in front. Each stride seems to take longer than in collection, with the moment of suspension being prolonged. There should be an impression that the horse spends more time in the air than on the ground.

To establish longer rather than higher strides, the rider allows the horse to lower and extend his neck a little. The rider who holds hard on to his horse reduces the freedom and suppleness: the horse's back tends to stiffen or even hollow so that just the legs flick back and forth and there can then be little spring to the pace.

On the other hand, the rider who simply lets the horse go by loosening the reins when trying to extend just allows him to fall on to his forehand (the forehand will then carry more weight). The horse will then be unable to move his shoulders freely and his steps will quicken rather than lengthen.

Impulsion

It is essential that the horse carries the majority of the weight with his hindquarters rather than his forehand, using his hindlegs actively and placing them well under his body. He must have impulsion, for he needs power to achieve these long strides. The hindquarters must be well engaged and the hindlegs active.

Some eye-catching extensions are seen when the forelegs are flicked high into the air while the hindlegs play little part in the proceedings. This is not a good extension, for again the back will be stiff and

Above Rinie Schaft and Juroen show how much longer the strides are in the extended trot than in either the medium or the collected trot. Although the strides are of a good length, ideally the outline could have been a little longer. The horse appears a little short in the neck.

Above Ulrich Lehmann extends his younger horse, Wörder. The strides are long but the horse seems to be having to balance himself a little on the reins. The result is that his head is behind the vertical and his neck has not been lowered and lengthened.

Above Reiner Klimke looks as if he might be in a little trouble. His young horse Ahlerich has tensed up and raised his head: one wrong move by the rider and the horse could lose his rhythm or even break into a canter. It will take positive, tactful riding to make him relax and lower his head into a position where the strides can become longer.

Above Wonderful, free, extended strides both in front and behind are being shown by the French chestnut gelding Vol au Vent. His rider M. Flament, from the Cadre Noir, has his seat in a driving position with his shoulders slightly behind the perpendicular.

Above This pair from Switzerland, Amy-Catherine de Bary and Aintree, demonstrate a controlled, active and free extended trot. The hindlegs are particularly well used with the hindleg coming as high off the ground as the foreleg. This means there will be no flicking of the forelegs.

Above Stephen Clarke and Ulysses from Great Britain make the extended trot look easy. The rider has persuaded his horse to take long, free, active strides without having to apply any obvious driving aids.

unable to co-ordinate the actions of the fore- and hindlegs. The horse cannot therefore be such a good gymnast, for he is only using part of his body.

Suppleness

Suppleness is essential to a good extension. The horse must be able to use every part of his body to produce the required long strides. When a horse is supple the strides will appear free and springy, rather than stiff and restricted.

Techniques

The skilful rider builds up the impulsion prior to the extension so that the horse has the power for the lengthening. But the rider only asks for as much extension as the horse can achieve without losing his balance. If he pushes too hard, or suddenly lets the reins go so that the horse transfers more of the weight on to his forehand, the horse will be forced to take shorter running steps.

As in the medium trot, it is better to ask for less and achieve even strides than to try for too much and lose it.

Differences

To earn good marks the lengthening should be visibly greater than in the medium trot. There must be a distinct difference between medium and extended paces. Some riders try a little cheating by going all out for the medium trot, establishing one that is good by general standards, but which is the longest their horse is capable of achieving. When they come to the extended movements they can do no better, and are consequently marked down.

Features	
Good	**Bad**
On the bit	Above/behind the bit
Outline lengthened	Head remains high, dips head down, short in neck
Rein contact light and constant	
Back supple, swinging	Pulling, no contact
Hindlegs as active as forelegs (cannon bones of hind- and forelegs parallel)	Hollow and stiff
	Flicking forelegs, dragging hindlegs
Strides long and elastic	Short, flat strides
Strides even in length	Uneven lengthening
Level, hindlegs used equally, and both forelegs	Unlevel
	Running
Rhythm pronounced and slow	

THE COLLECTED CANTER

The canter, with its potential to achieve greater speed and the bounding nature of each stride, enables more impulsion to be produced than in the other paces. It is the most exciting and the most powerful of the dressage paces. In show-jumping it is used in preference to the trot or gallop to jump high fences.

Straightness

The sequence of the footfalls is a symmetrical, unlike the walk and trot (see glossary). This makes it difficult to keep the horse straight, with the hindquarters tending to swing to the side of the leading leg. Straightness is essential to build up impulsion (see glossary) so that in canter work riders are constantly having to combat the natural tendency of the horse to swing his hindquarters inwards.

Rhythm

The other vital consideration in the canter is to maintain that pronounced three-time rhythm. If the hindlegs are not kept active there is a tendency for the horse to fall into a four-time rhythm (the outside foreleg moves before the inside hindleg). If this happens the canter becomes flatter, with less, if any, spring and the important moment of suspension is lost or minimized.

Cadence

The canter strides should be light and have cadence. Cadence, a fashionable word in modern dressage, means that the rhythm of the pace is pronounced and slow; that there is spring to the pace. Cadence can only be produced if the hindquarters are well engaged and active, and able to provide the power

Above Feuerball from Germany shows a lovely, round collected canter with short, active and high strides. The outline is good with the head and neck being well-raised. A shortcoming might be that Dr Klimke has no rein contact; this was probably a momentary release after he had applied a half halt to ensure the horse was carrying himself and not balancing on the reins.

Above Anne d'Ieteren from Belgium in collected canter. Although quite relaxed, Juroto appears a little too heavy in the hands. There is not the lightness of the forehand seen in really good collection, and this might be due to the horse having lost his balance on the turn.

Above Another stage in Anne d'Ieteren and Juroto's collected canter across the arena. They have improved the outline but they are not showing as much collection as Feuerball and Dr Klimke in the earlier picture. Juroto's hindquarters are not so well engaged as Feuerball's, but Dr Klimke was probably super-collecting his horse prior to the halt.

Above Chris Bartle and Wily Trout in a pleasing collected canter. The horse's head and neck are slightly bent to the inside (towards the leading leg). The rider's weight is slightly to the inside.

for the horse to spring off the ground. Horses which have cadence have great impulsion and appear very gymnastic. Much impulsion has to be generated to create cadence, but it should not be obtained at the expense of lightness and fluency.

The premium on cadence is one of the reasons for the popularity of the powerful Continental breeds. They have much more natural spring to their paces, and greater power in their hindquarters, than the thoroughbred. The latter, although more elegant, tends to have strides which are longer and flatter (they were after all bred to gallop as fast as possible, to take long flat strides rather than springy, athletic steps).

Cadence also puts the emphasis on gymnastic – rather than ballet-like – dressage. It makes dressage more exciting and dramatic to watch, but some competitors produce cadence at the cost of elegance and lightness.

The collection

In the collected canter the cadence should abound, but this will only be possible if the horse is ridden forward into collection and not slowed down with

Above Dr Klimke and Ahlerich show an excellent collected canter through a corner. The strides are so short and balanced that he is practically able to go into the right angle. Note, too, the excellent position of the forehand, with the head and the neck well raised.

Above Frances Verbeek-van Rooy and Ivar are in collected canter as they go down the centre line. The horse looks relaxed and alert, but his strides are longer and not so high as Feuerball's. The horse appears under control and ready for any movement that may be asked of him.

the reins (as at the collected trot and walk). The hindquarters should become more active and slightly lowered, the head should rise and the neck become more arched.

With the bounding nature of the pace and the definite period of suspension, the lightening of the forehand in collection results in even greater freedom and mobility of the shoulders than at the walk and trot.

Use in tests

As in the trot, a great deal of use is made of the collected version of the canter. The greater mobility means that movements can be performed out of it. The horse is therefore in collected canter for pirouettes, half pass, counter canter and most of the changes. It is a vital pace for a dressage horse.

Features	
Good	**Bad**
On the bit	Above/behind the bit
Outline shortened	Outline too long
Head vertical	Behind or in front of vertical
Neck raised and arched	
Hindquarters very active and slightly lowered	Head and neck too low
	Trudging, dragging hindquarters
Strides elevated and short with distinct suspension	Flat, longish strides
Strides light and cadenced	Heavy strides
Hoofbeats regular with pronounced three-time	Four-time hoofbeats, irregular
Sequence maintained and united	Disunited

THE MEDIUM CANTER

As in the medium trot, the requirements of the medium canter are good lengthening of the strides and slight lowering of the neck from the collected position, with the head just in front of the vertical.

Even, unhurried strides

Again, the essence is to achieve strides of an even length with powerful and active use of the hindquarters so that the weight does not fall on to the forehand. As soon as the horse goes on to his forehand, he will find it difficult to lengthen his strides, and if pushed he will simply start to quicken and run.

With most horses, even strides are easier to establish at the canter than at the trot. This is partly because it is easier for the rider to sit softly 'with' the horse in the canter. Then the horse is less likely to stiffen against the rider; his back will remain supple and so maintain that vital bridge for impulsion between the hindquarters and the forehand. The motion of the trot is greater through the horse's back so that the rider finds it more difficult to absorb the movement with his lower back. He is all too easily bounced up and down (especially in extensions), which is painful for the horse and makes him stiffen his back, lose impulsion and quicken rather than lengthen his stride.

Straightness

The medium canter is more difficult than the trot in one way, and that is in keeping the horse straight. Unless the rider takes positive action to encourage the horse to put his inside hindleg (the hindleg on the side of the leading leg) well forward, and to stop the outside shoulder from falling out, the horse will naturally tend to curl his hindquarters to the inside.

To check that this does not occur, the medium canter is asked for in straight lines, usually along the long side of the arena, where the judges can see if the hindquarters swing inwards.

Features	
Good	**Bad**
On the bit	Above/behind the bit
Head just in front of vertical	Head vertical or behind it
Neck lower, less arched than in collection	Neck too high or too low
Hindquarters well engaged, active	On the forehand
Strides of medium extension	Strides too short or long
Strides even, balanced and free	Hurried, uneven strides, restricted and stiff
Hoofbeats regular	Loss of rhythm, lack of cadence
Pronounced three-time rhythm with distinct moment of suspension	

Above Granat's medium canter shows good lengthening of strides without losing the spring. However, on this occasion it seems to have taken effort on the part of his rider, Christine Stückelberger, to produce the medium canter.

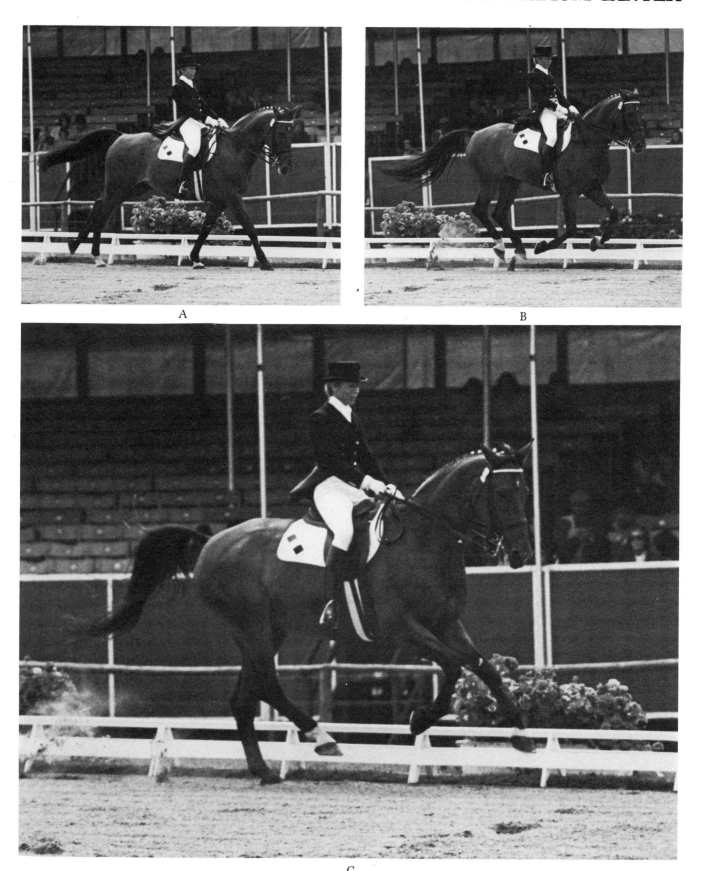

A

B

C

Above A sequence of three shots showing Mme Otto-Crépin and Don Giovanni from France performing the medium canter down the long side of the arena in an exemplary and elegant fashion. The horse has lengthened his outline and stride without losing his bounce, for in the moment of suspension he is well off the ground. This sequence also shows the considerable change in the level of the horse at the canter. Prior to the moment of suspension (**A**) the horse's head and neck are much higher than just afterwards (**B**). The rider, as Mme Otto-Crépin demonstrates, must be very supple in the lower back to remain upright.

THE EXTENDED CANTER

At the extended canter the horse lengthens his strides to the utmost without falling into the four-time beat of the gallop. It is important that the moment of suspension remains clearly visible, and that the horse does not flatten out and his strides become heavy. The hindquarters must remain well engaged so that the extended canter is achieved by using the driving aids of the seat and legs and not simply letting him go in front.

The rider needs to ease the rein contact just enough to allow the horse to lower his head and neck slightly, and for the head to come a little more in front of the vertical.

Calmness

The urging forward to achieve those extended strides must not be at the expense of calmness. The horse must remain relaxed and able to take strides of an even length.

Each stride should take a relatively long time. It is of no value if the horse is pushed faster so that the strides become quicker and shorter.

Straightness

The difficulty of keeping the horse straight, discussed under the heading 'Medium Canter', still holds. The rider has to take positive action bringing the fore-hand to the inside of the track to ensure that the hindquarters do not curve to the inside.

Features	
Good	**Bad**
On the bit	Above/behind the bit
Head lower and in front of the vertical	Head too high, behind vertical
Strides lengthened to their utmost	Strides restricted
Strides balanced, even, long and slow	Hurried, uneven, short, quick strides
Hoofbeats regular with three-time rhythm and suspension pronounced	Flat, irregular strides
Calm	Tense, pulling

Above Mme Otto-Crépin and Don Giovanni give another excellent demonstration of free lengthening of the strides at the canter. This time she has asked her forward-going horse to lower and lengthen his outline a little more in order to achieve extended, rather than medium, strides.

Above left Ulrich Lehmann asks Wörder to extend his strides across the diagonal. Although appearing calm and relaxed, the horse is not so light in the hand nor has he as much spring or length to the stride as in the previous picture. **Above right** Chris Bartle and Wily Trout extend across the diagonal. There is good lengthening of the stride, and active use of the hindlegs. This will ensure that the canter keeps its bounce and power, and does not flatten. However, the head and neck could have been more extended. **Below** Uwe Schulten-Baumer shows great concentration as he persuades Slibovitz to produce this pleasing extension. He displays clearly the pronounced aids necessary to ensure that the forehand is slightly bent towards the leading leg, and that the hindquarters do not swing to the inside.

THE COUNTER CANTER

The canter is an asymmetrical pace with the fore- and hindleg on one side leading to come down further forward than the limbs on the other side. The horse finds it easier to canter a circle when the leading legs are on the inside, and this is known as a 'true canter'. It is, however, a test of obedience, suppleness and balance for the horse to canter with the outside leg leading (that is, on a right circle, with the left leading) and this is known as the counter canter.

Bend
The horse should maintain the same bend when in counter canter (that is, it is bent towards the side of the leading leg, and not to the inside of the circle). This bend should only be slight. It is quite common for a horse to curl his hindquarters to the side of his leading leg when he must start to move on two tracks (that is, with the hindlegs no longer following in the tracks of the forelegs).

Use in tests
In the international tests the counter canter is performed at the collected version of the canter. It is asked for in serpentines (see page 66), the loops of which are much smaller and therefore more difficult in the Intermédiaire I and Intermédiaire II than in the Prix St Georges.

The trickiest part of the serpentines in international tests occurs at X. The horse approaches it in the counter canter, and then as he changes direction at X he has to complete a flying change into the opposite counter canter. Performing a flying change from counter canter into the opposite counter canter demands great obedience and suppleness, for it is against the natural approach of the horse to change into anything other than the true canter.

Rhythm
In the counter canter the horse still has to maintain the purity of the pace (cadence, rhythm, even strides etc.). To do this in the small loops of the serpentine in the Intermédiaire I and Intermédiaire II demands considerable collection and suppleness.

Features	
Good	**Bad**
On the bit	Above/behind the bit
Bent slightly towards leading leg	Straight in neck or bent to inside of turn
Hindlegs follow tracks of forelegs	Hindquarters swinging
Strides even	Inconsistent strides
Strides cadenced, light and united	Flat, heavy, disunited
Hoofbeats in regular three-time rhythm	Four-time rhythm

A

B

C

E

D

Petra Cox and Little Diamond from Holland performing one of the difficult loops of a serpentine, which must be taken at counter canter with the outside leg leading. In **A** she has achieved a good deal of collection, which will be necessary for the small radius of the loop. In **B** the horse still looks relaxed and balanced in this more difficult position. In **C** they are starting to turn but, ideally, they should have gone a little further to reach the track. In **D** there should have been a little more bend towards the leading leg – a good indication of suppleness. In **E** although this is the moment in the canter when the horse tips forward (see medium canter), Little Diamond has gone a little too far, with his head coming behind the vertical and putting too much weight on his forehand. By **F** the rider has worked for more engagement of the hindquarters, and the head and neck have come up into a better position.

F

THE REIN BACK

In the rein back the horse moves backwards lifting each foreleg just in advance of its diagonal hindleg (that is, moving almost simultaneously the diagonal pair of a fore- and hindleg). Four hoofbeats can just be heard, but as in the walk the intervals are not equal: a long interval is followed by a short, then another long and short interval.

Technique

The term rein back is misleading, for if the reins are the main means of asking the horse to step backwards he will resist, usually by raising or lowering his head, stiffening his back and dragging his feet. To produce a good rein back, the reins merely restrain the horse from going forward; once again the driving aids must initiate the action.

The leg and seat aids are applied and as the horse starts to think of going forwards he is restrained, but not pulled, by the reins, and the only route is backwards. The result of this method is that the hindlegs are activated and lifted well into the air. Similarly the forelegs should be well flexed when lifted, and this is best achieved if the weight is not on the forehand.

Straightness

The legs should move straight back so that the hindquarters do not swing to one side. Therefore both hindlegs must be equally active, taking the same size of step.

The steps themselves, should be free and each one of an even length. Choppy, quick short steps do not earn good marks.

Use in tests

The rein back is asked for after a halt has been established, but thereafter variations occur. A specified number of steps are required (between four and six), and after taking them the horse must move forward without hesitation into the required movement. This might be a trot, canter, passage or even a specified number of walk steps forward before again being asked for another rein back. This forward, back and forward movement is demanding not only for the rider, who must count very carefully to get the number of steps right, but also for the horse, for whom it is exceptionally difficult to keep the movement smooth and fluent.

The horse must be very supple and obedient if he is to take steps of equal size forward and backward, and to transfer smoothly from a forward to a backward momentum. The rider must rely on the seat and legs to achieve this and not pull on the reins.

Features	
Good	**Bad**
On the bit	Above/behind the bit
Hindlegs and forelegs moved in almost simultaneous diagonal pairs	Hoofbeats evenly interspaced
Outline remains round with back supple	Stiffens and/or hollows back
Strides straight, relatively high, even, active	Spreads hindlegs, inactive, drags forelegs, shuffles

A

C

Opposite Uwe Schulten-Baumer and Slibovitz can make high-class transitions between reining back, going forward, back and finally forward again in this tricky movement. The picture indicates why they do it so well. The horse is going back in response to the rider's seat and leg aids, for the rein contact, although constant, is light and the rider is not pulling. The horse has also remained in a good outline, without resisting. **Above and right** Cindy Neale and Martyr have been Canada's most successful combination in the late 1970s. These pictures show them going back (**A**), forwards (**B**) and back again (**C**). To do this well, the direction of the momentum must change, and there should be a slight transfer of weight distribution. In **A** it can be seen that the hindquarters are lowered and the horse is carrying a good deal of weight on them. In **B**, with the forward momentum, the weight has gone forwards. It is obvious that the reins are not being used to ask him to come back.

THE SHOULDER-IN

The shoulder-in probably is the most valuable of all the movements in the training of the horse. It was discovered by the great French horsemaster de Guérinière in the early eighteenth century and provided an exercise which promotes collection, suppleness and straightness.

Benefits

The shoulder-in is a suppling and straightening exercise. The horse moves sideways when slightly bent around the inside leg of the rider. NB Inside is always the direction to which the horse is bent (see Glossary).

The shoulder-in stretches the muscles to the outside, softens the muscles to the inside, and the use of the shoulder-in to the left and right encourages the horse to use his muscles evenly on both sides. By

nature, every horse has one side which is stiff and the other which is supple, just as we are right- or left-handed. In training, the rider has to choose exercises which will enable the horse to use both sides evenly, and the shoulder-in is the best of these.

The shoulder-in is also an exercise that promotes collection, as the horse must move his inside hindleg underneath his body to place it to the side but in front of the outside hind. To do this correctly he must lower his inside hip (on his inside hindquarter), and thus lower and engage his hindquarters; this is the essence of collection.

Technique

In the shoulder-in the forehand is brought off the track to make an angle to it of about 30 degrees. The hindlegs are kept on the original track (usually the

Opposite left The horse must be balanced, collected and very supple to achieve an angle of 30 degrees in the shoulder-in. Things often go wrong in tests and these vital factors are lost – the horse stiffens and is reluctant to obey. The result can be as seen here, where the forehand is barely brought off the track. **Opposite right** The shoulder-in is performed to the right and the left. In the series on page 101 Uwe Sauer and Montevideo are in right shoulder-in. In this left shoulder in they are at a slightly smaller angle to the centre line than on the other rein. **Above** A shoulder-in viewed from alongside. Although a satisfactory shoulder-in the horse is relying a little on the reins for balance and tilting his head slightly. More weight could be carried by the hindquarters.

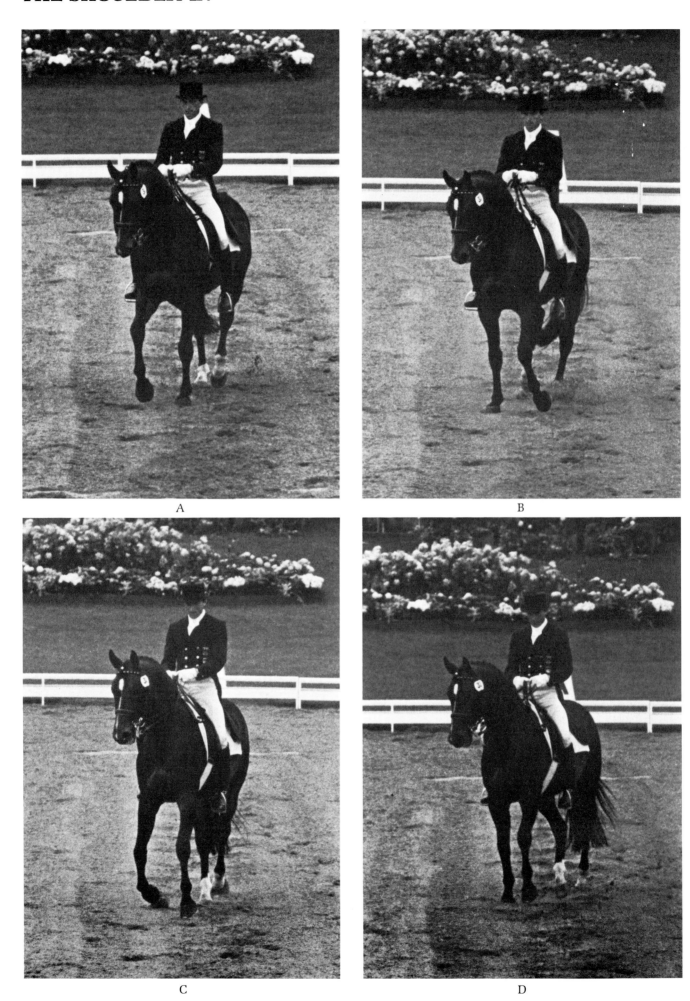

A

B

C

D

Uwe Sauer shows some good shoulder-in down the centre line on the stallion, Montevideo. He is at about the correct angle of 30 degrees to the centre line, although he does lose it slightly in **B** with the forehand coming closer to the centre line. It can be seen that the hindlegs are remaining on the original track, moving straight ahead but with the inside hindleg just turned slightly. As the forehand comes off the track, the forelegs may actually cross, as they are about to do in **E**. The horse should remain slightly bent around the rider's inside leg (Uwe Sauer's right leg). Sometimes there is some tilting of the head (a fault) and this is just starting to happen in **E**. Compare **E** with **D**, where the horse is in an excellent position. Montevideo is not relying on the reins for balance and he has his head and his neck raised and arched.

E

centre line in international tests, and the long side of the arena in early training). The whole horse is therefore slightly bent around the rider's inside leg, which means he will be turned away from the direction in which he is moving.

As he moves, the inside foreleg passes and crosses in front of the outside foreleg; the inside hindleg is placed in front of the outside hindleg. This crossing over of the limbs is termed lateral work.

The bend

The position of the horse in the shoulder-in (that is, slightly bent around the rider's inside leg) is the same as that required on a circle. There should not be excessive bend in the neck, for then the outside shoulder is pushed out and it is difficult to maintain impulsion when a horse is excessively bent.

On the other hand the horse should not be absolutely straight, for then he will simply cross his hindlegs (as in leg yield) and not lower his inside hip, which is the vital action if the shoulder-in is to help collection.

The steps

The strides in the shoulder-in should be of equal size, just as free and regular as in the collected trot prior to it. There must be no shortening, stiffening or unevenness as the horse starts to go sideways. The horse should glide fluently from going straight to moving sideways.

Positioning

The horse must keep his hindlegs on the original track, and maintain the same angle to it (ideally 30 degrees) with his forehand, throughout the movement. This is particularly difficult to achieve when performed on the centre line (as in international tests), as there is then no solid base, wall or boards to work from.

Judges' comments about the shoulder-in frequently include 'wavering', 'changing angle' and 'not remaining on the track' as to position correctly takes a balanced horse and skilful riding.

Features	
Good	**Bad**
On the bit	Above/behind the bit
Bend slight and to inside	Too straight or too bent
Forehand maintains angle 30 degrees to track	Angle varying, forehand remains on track
Hindquarters active and remain on the track	Dragging hindquarters, coming off track, hindquarters pushed out
Outline round and supple	
Strides even, level, free, regular, cadenced	Hollows back, stiff
	Loss of impulsion, rhythm, freedom
	Strides flat

RENVERS AND TRAVERS

These are slightly easier versions of the half pass which, instead of being performed across the diagonal or to either side of the centre line, are performed along the long side, or in international tests down the centre line. The major difference is that the horse is not parallel to the long side in the renvers or travers but at an angle of about 30 degrees to it.

Technique

The bend in the horse's body and the direction in which he is looking are identical to those in the half pass (that is, slightly bent around the rider's inside leg, and looking in the direction towards which he is moving). The difference is that in the case of the travers the forelegs stay on the track or centre line,

A

B

C

D

and for the renvers the hindlegs do (that is, in travers the head is towards the track, and in renvers the tail, and for this reason they are sometimes called head-to-wall and tail-to-wall respectively).

The aim in both renvers and travers should be to keep the horse at an angle of about 30 degrees in the direction towards which he is moving. The same features demanded of the half pass hold for renvers and travers (that is, long free strides, mobility of shoulders etc). ·

Use in tests

In the international tests renvers and travers are performed on the centre line, therefore many of the problems are the same as for shoulder-in (that is, angle varying, feet coming off the track and not enough angle).

*Uwe Sauer and Montevideo once again give an excellent demonstration of a movement. This time it is the renvers, one of the least common dressage movements. The horse's direction is not perfect, for the hindlegs should be on the centre line. In this case they never quite reached it but otherwise the effect is impressive. The horse is distinctly bent around the rider's inside leg. Uwe Sauer's leg can be seen to give a strong aid at times **A**, and relaxed at others **C**. This is the leg which keeps up the impulsion, as well as acting as a support for the bend. Therefore, the rider needs to vary its use according to whether the horse is getting lazy, too impetuous or stiffening. To do this well requires 'feel' – that ability which distinguishes great horsemen when a rider can anticipate his horse's error and correct it before it occurs.*

Above Once things start going wrong it is difficult to restore the equilibrium, and the same rider who was in trouble over the shoulder-in is having difficulties in the renvers. The horse's hindlegs have gone over the centre line. The forehand is barely at 30 degrees to the line, there is a lack of bend in the body and the horse is tilting his head which means he is trying to evade some of the aids.

E

Features	
Good	**Bad**
On the bit	Above/behind the bit
Rein contact light	Tilting head, short in neck
Forelegs (travers), hindlegs (renvers) remain on track	Coming off track
	On forehand, restricted
Shoulders free	Dragging hindquarters, unlevel
Hindquarters active, engaged, level	Wrong bend, excessive bend restricting impulsion, too straight
Bend slight but distinct	
Angle 30 degrees maintained	Angle varying
Strides even, free and cadenced	Uneven, restricted, stiff

THE HALF PASS AT TROT

The half pass is the prettiest of the lateral work, and in some cases can be quite breathtaking. This is so in the case of the Olympic champion Granat, whose strides in half pass are so long, and have such spring, that he barely touches the ground. Granat provides an exhibition of extraordinary power, suppleness and impulsion. Every dressage rider must long for the opportunity to ride, feel and control that great gymnastic energy. Other horses appear earthbound in comparison. The half pass gives the horse the opportunity to show off his suppleness, impulsion and balance in a spectacular manner as she moves forwards and sideways at the same time.

Technique

In the half pass the horse is slightly bent around the rider's inside leg and looks towards the direction he is moving (the opposite to the shoulder-in). It is important that the forehand leads the hindquarters, but only just, as the body should be as close as possible parallel to the long side. The horse's outside legs pass and cross in front of the inside ones. The amount of crossing (lateral action) becomes greater as the tests become more difficult. In the Grand Prix the angle for the half pass is twice as great as in the Prix St Georges, the horse having to half pass across the whole arena before the centre instead of just half (that is, F to E in Grand Prix, F to X in Prix St Georges).

Strides

The horse can get across the arena in half pass by

Above Lady Joicey and Sascha from Great Britain had much less experience internationally than most of the other competitors at the Festival. Nevertheless, they put up pleasing performances. In this half pass the horse is happily submitting to his work although he could show more bend.

Above An eye-catching back view of the half pass. Note the identical positions of the hooves of the hind- and fore-leg diagonal. The amount of crossing of the legs shows great suppleness. The horse is almost parallel to the long side, i.e. the hindquarters are neither trailing nor leading and the head is slightly bent to the left.

Above This pair is shown at a bad moment. The horse is probably finding it difficult to get far enough sideways, his hindquarters have started to trail behind him and he has lost the bend to the inside (the way of going). Despite the difficulties the rider has maintained a good position which should help the horse to improve this half pass.

Above Anne-Grethe Jensen and Marzog, the attractive Danish pair, in another interesting aspect of the half pass. When viewed from the side the distinct bend of the head and neck (but with no tilting of the head) can be clearly seen. The strong use of the rider's inside leg is also obvious.

taking short strides, but more marks are gained, and it looks so much more graceful, if the strides are long, free and cadenced. This requires suppleness, and engagement of hindquarters to provide impulsion. Weight can then be taken off the forehand, and the shoulders become more mobile and free – and more able to take elevated sweeping strides.

In the collected trot just prior to a half pass, riders usually try to build up an extra store of impulsion (through half halts). Then they release a little of this energy in the movement itself to enable the horse to glide (rather than struggle) across the arena. In the well prepared half pass the rider has little work to do during the movement itself.

Above Uwe Schulten-Baumer and Slibovitz glide across the arena in a half pass. The horse is taking those much sought-after long, free strides. He is bent slightly to the way of going and the hindlegs are clearly crossing over.

A

B

Bonnie Bonnello and Satchmo performing a sheer half pass to the left changing at arena point X to an equally sheer half pass to the right. In **A** the rider asks the horse to change his bend and direction of movement. A few strides later in **B**, she has not yet established a really good bend to the right. The centre of gravity is behind the direction of the movement and there is too much weight on the horse's left shoulder. The result is that the horse is finding it difficult to get across and has tilted his head. By **C** the balance is improving.

C

Features	
Good	**Bad**
On the bit	Above/behind the bit
Rein contact light	Tilting head, pulling, short in the neck
Shoulders free	
Hindlegs active, well engaged and level strides	On the forehand
	Dragging hind legs
	Unlevel
Body almost parallel to long side, but forehand just in lead	Hindquarters trailing or leading
Bend slight but distinct	No bend, wrong bend, excessive bend, restricting forward momentum
Strides even, free and cadenced	Uneven, restricted, stiff strides
Rhythm pronounced two-time	Loss of two-time rhythm

THE HALF PASS AT CANTER

Use in tests

The half pass is the only lateral movement asked for at the canter in international tests. In these tests the canter half pass is complicated because it is asked for in a zigzag or counter-change of hand: the horse is asked for a canter half pass in one direction which is followed immediately by a half pass in the opposite direction. As this is done at the canter there is the added difficulty of having to complete a flying change before changing the direction.

In the Prix St Georges the counter change of hand at the canter is relatively simple. The competitor half passes from the centre line to the half-way marker on the long side (B or E), changing leg and then half passing back to the centre line.

The zigzag

In the more difficult tests, a series of counter-changes of hand are asked for down the centre line, which is then known as a zigzag. To make it even more difficult, a specified number of strides are asked for on either side of the centre line. Not only has the rider to establish a half pass featuring all the good points discussed under the trot half pass, but after a certain number of strides he has to straighten his horse (prior to this the forehand should be just leading), prepare and ask for the change, ensure that the new bend is established, that the forehand is leading, and then ask for a good half pass in the opposite direction. The competitor then completes the required number of strides before repeating.

A

B

In the following sequence of pictures Amy-Catherine de Bary and Aintree from Switzerland show the tricky change in direction required in the canter zigzag. In **A** they are in

a good half pass to the right. In **B** Miss de Bary starts to straighten Aintree, asking him to bring his hindquarters further over to the right so that his forehand is no longer in

The rider has to be quick-thinking, sensitive to problems which will restrict fluency (e.g. the hindquarters trailing) and have excellent timing to apply the aids just at the right moment. The horse must be exceptionally supple if he is to change the bend smoothly and achieve the angle of the half pass.

In the Grand Prix it is particularly difficult, as five counter-changes of hand have to be fitted in down the centre line, starting with a half pass of three strides, followed by four of six strides, and finishing back on the centre line after a half pass of three strides.

When this movement is done well the horse swings fluently from side to side and keeps up a great rhythm: this makes it very graceful to watch.

Features	
Good	**Bad**
On the bit	Above/behind the bit
Head straight	Tilting head
Straight in change	Crooked change, swinging hindquarters
Forehand just in lead	Hindquarters trailing or hindquarters leading
Bend slight but distinctive	No bend or too much
Correct number of strides	Too many/too few strides
Strides cadenced and free	Strides restricted and short
Passes even amounts on either side	Sideways more in one direction than other

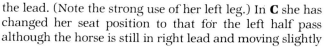

C

D

the lead. (Note the strong use of her left leg.) In **C** she has changed her seat position to that for the left half pass although the horse is still in right lead and moving slightly

right. (Note the angle of the left foreleg.) In **D** she has started to give her aids to change to the left leg. (Note her right leg has gone back and her left leg forward.)

A

Cindy Neale and Equus perform a canter zigzag. In **A** they have just changed from the right to the left lead and moved into the left half pass. It is not a very balanced change for Equus has fallen on to his forehand and is overbending slightly. They recover quickly for in **B** they are in a pleasing half pass to the left with the forehand correctly in the lead. In **C** Cindy Neale has started to straighten Equus in preparation for the change. In **D** he makes a good change to the right with a distinct bend to the new lead. By **E** the bend has been more clearly established.

THE PIROUETTE

The pirouette is a tiny circle with a radius ideally no larger than the length of the horse. It is a variation of a lateral movement in that the forelegs cross to move laterally, so that the forehand moves around the hindquarters. The hindlegs remain almost on the spot and are simply lifted up and down. The inside hindleg is the pivot point, but it must not be a stationary pivot, it should be lifted up and put down in the same place or slightly in front. The outside hindleg moves around it.

The horse's body is slightly bent to the direction in which he is turning, and he should move around smoothly, maintaining the rhythm and sequence of the pace.

Versions

The pirouette is performed at walk and canter in the international competitions, and is an excellent test of the degree of collection at these paces. The collection must be very good indeed if the horse is to keep his hindlegs moving yet in almost the same place.

When the horse keeps his hindquarters in the same place at the trot he is in the piaffe (see page 126), hence the trot pirouette can only be performed in piaffe. This is a very difficult movement which is only possible for horses which have mastered the supreme dressage movement of piaffe. It is not asked for in tests, but the maestros use it to show off the brilliance of their horses in the Free Style competitions.

At the walk it is usual to ask only for a half pirouette – a turn through 180 degrees (as opposed to 360 degrees).

Technique at the walk

The preparation for the pirouette is vital, for only a horse which is very collected can keep his hindlegs marching almost on the spot. He should not simply swivel round pivoting on the inside hindleg, nor must he swing his hindquarters to the outside or move forward to perform a small circle rather than a pirouette.

The rider must create and contain the impulsion so that the horse can turn smoothly on the spot. Usually, therefore, riders half halt frequently prior to the pirouette, establish a slight bend to the direction of turning and then ask for the pirouette, which should be moved into fluently without hesitation or resistance to the rein contact.

The four-time marching rhythm and the sequence of the walk must be maintained so that the horse neither stops, trots nor ambles, and this requires plenty of impulsion.

Nor must the horse step backwards. This is considered a much more serious fault than stepping forwards. It is a basic premise of good training that the horse should be willing and able to go forward (not backwards) at all times: a forward going horse is also easier for the rider to direct.

Above Mrs Tove Jorck Jorckston and Lazuly from Denmark performed attractive tests. In this half pirouette they are showing a good amount of bend. Lazuly is remaining on the bit, the forelegs are taking free, long strides while the hindlegs remain close together.

Features	
Good	**Bad**
On the bit	Above/behind the bit
Bend slightly to inside	Straight or wrong bend
Hindlegs lifted and returned almost to same spot	Hindquarters swing out, or move backwards
Strides free and even in front, level behind	Short restricted strides, unlevel
Rhythm regular, sequence maintained	Swivels, does not maintain four-time rhythm and true sequence
Collected	Falling on to forehand

A

B

C

D

E

Bonnie Bonnello and Satchmo from Canada are walking into this half pirouette with a little less collection than is necessary to make it easy. The steps are not quite high and short enough and they will run into problems. In **A** she asks for a bend to the right. In **B** the horse has started to move his forehand around but he is not relaxed and resists by tilting his head. His hindlegs are far apart which means he cannot take the short steps behind needed to keep his forehand moving freely around. The result in **C** is that he is very unbalanced, and his forelegs seem to have stopped moving – which will mean a loss of rhythm. In **D** he has restored his balance and in **E** the picture is pleasing. In **D** and **E** the horse is nicely on the bit; the forelegs are taking longer strides around the hindlegs which keep moving almost on the spot.

THE CANTER PIROUETTE

A canter pirouette is one of the most exacting of the dressage movements. To achieve sufficient control, collection and impulsion to enable the horse to reduce his natural canter speed of about 10–15 mph to almost 0 mph takes years of training and considerable talent. Nor is it of any value in dressage to try the easier method and, as in polo, simply swing the forehand around the stationary pivoting hindlegs. This swivel still takes training, but with a sharp bit and an athletic pony it can be done quickly.

In dressage the purity (sequence and rhythm) of the paces is basic to the sport. The rhythm and sequence of the canter has therefore to be maintained in all canter work. This makes everything appear for spectators, and feel for riders, more fluent and supple; but it is very difficult to achieve, especially in the pirouette, in which the horse has to canter with his hindlegs almost on the spot.

Technique

The essence of a good canter pirouette is to be able to start in a very, very slow collected canter which is abounding with vital energy (impulsion). Then, with the hindquarters slightly lowered, the horse is bent slightly towards the direction in which he is to turn. As long as the hindquarters are very well engaged his forehand is light and free, and he will be able to move the latter around his hindquarters.

As in the walk pirouettes, the horse should not move backwards, swing his hindquarters or lose the regularity of the three-time rhythm of the canter. Most young horses find this very difficult and either lose the impulsion and fall back into the trot or walk. Other horses try to use speed rather than impulsion to move around, attempting to complete the pirouette in one or two strides. A horse which does this is said to swivel.

A

B

E

F

The strides should be small, supple bounds, not stiff, staccato movements. If he lifts so high that the strides become small rears, much of the impulsion is lost; if he takes flat, laborious strides, he lacks impulsion and will find it very difficult to perform a pirouette rather than a small circle.

The strides, too, should be of an equal size. This means the horse must remain balanced and this greatly depends on the ability of the rider to remain in balance with the horse. The rider must keep his weight squarely in the saddle so as not to disturb the horse. This is not very easy at times when the horse turns very quickly or needs a great deal of pushing to keep up the impulsion to move around.

The strides must not be so large that the pirouette turns into the swivel of polo ponies. The horse should take, ideally, between six and eight strides to complete a full pirouette.

In **A**, Uwe Schulten-Baumer is super-collecting Slibovitz and asking for a bend in the direction of the pirouette. In **B** the forehand has started to come around and the rider is applying his outside leg strongly. **C** shows the immense collection this horse has achieved – he is light in the hand and his hindlegs are far under his body. **D** is the moment in the canter when the horse tips forward as his legs return to the ground after the moment of suspension. The rider is giving the horse strong assistance to restore the lighter position when the hindlegs carry more of the weight. In **E** the rider has brought his own body closer to the perpendicular again. **F** is a similar position to **D** but viewed from the rear. In **G** we are able to see the strong support given to the horse by the rider's inside leg and in **H** there is that pleasing picture of lightness and self-carriage again. This sequence shows the considerable adjustment needed on the part of the rider and horse to complete a pirouette.

C

D

G

H

A

B

Above Two stages in the pirouette of the Dane Finn Larsen on his Swedish horse Coq d'Or. In **A** the rider is just starting the movement. The horse appears quite strong in the hand but he has a good outline and the hocks are well engaged. Note how much weight the rider is putting to the inside; many other riders remain central, and some even put the weight on the outside. This distribution of weight in the pirouette is one aspect of dressage in which techniques vary. In **B** this same pair show a very good moment in a pirouette where the impression is one of great control and manoeuvrability. This pirouette must have been completed in a very small space indeed.

Above Uwe Sauer is one of the maestros at canter pirouettes. He has great ability to collect his horse and this picture of his Trakehner cross thoroughbred, Hirtentraum, shows excellent engagement of the hindquarters, a good bend in the body and a great ease of movement.

Above Christine Stückelberger and Granat also show good engagement of the hindquarters but Granat has wandered off the centre line. However, it is better to make a larger pirouette in a good canter rhythm showing good collection than to make a small pirouette and lose these features.

Above Canter pirouettes demand great collection, balance and unison between horse and rider. With these requirements many mistakes are seen in this movement. In this picture the horse has probably swung around faster than anticipated and momentarily lost balance.

Use in tests

The full pirouette is first asked for in the Intermédiaire I. For horses at an earlier stage of training, in the Prix St Georges, the easier half pirouette is required, and in these three or four strides is considered ideal.

Where the pirouette is performed also determines its degree of difficulty. For example, in the Prix St Georges it is performed anywhere between two points on the diagonal between F and X and between K and X. The rider may pick his place within these limits, and, if the hindlegs do not remain almost on the same spot, it is difficult for the judges to detect, as they view it from the side rather than from behind or in front. In the Grand Prix Special, on the other hand, the pirouettes have to be done at an exact point and on the centre line. This is much more difficult as the rider has to time his preparation exactly, and if the hindlegs deviate off the centre line this is obvious to the judges.

The 'greats'

It is magnificent to watch the 'greats' perform pirouettes. Uwe Sauer from Germany has the ability to collect his horse so much beforehand – to get him to lower his hindquarters and almost canter on the spot – that the pirouettes then become easy. The Olympic silver medallists Harry Boldt and Woyceck created all the necessary power very easily and their performance was fluent, effortless and very elegant.

The canter pirouette requires exceptional suppleness and muscle power. It is very exciting to see riders trying to get their horses to build up and contain all the necessary power, and beautiful when they can do so apparently without effort. This is only possible with great co-operation from the horses, which must try their utmost in this manoeuvre.

Features	
Good	**Bad**
On the bit	Above/behind the bit
Back supple and round	Hollow/stiff back
Hindquarters exceptionally well engaged	Head coming high without engagement behind
Hindquarters active but remaining almost on the spot	Swinging hindquarters, moving backwards, small circle
Bent in direction of movement	Wrong bend, not enough bend
Strides supple, light, cadenced and even	Heavy, laboured, stiff, flat or rearing strides
Strides number 6–8 in a whole pirouette, 3–4 in half pirouette	Swivels around in 1 or 2 strides or tiny, stiff strides
Rhythm regular, purity of canter maintained	Sequence and rhythm of canter lost. Walks, trots

THE FLYING CHANGE

At the canter the asymmetrical manner in which the horse moves his legs results in his leading with either the left or right legs. Novice horses change leading legs by coming back to the walk or trot (a simple change). As training advances, the horse becomes more obedient to the aids, the canter gains more collection, cadence, balance and activity, and at this stage it is possible for him to change the lead during the moment of suspension when all the legs are off the ground (a flying change).

A correct change

Simply changing the leading foreleg is possible for a novice but the horse will be disunited (on a different leading leg behind from in front) and will therefore be unbalanced. For this reason, he must learn to change both behind and in front, but it is difficult to change behind unless the horse uses his hindlegs actively and has his hindquarters engaged; thus the need for basic training before teaching the flying change.

The change of legs behind and in front has to be completed simultaneously. A competitor will be marked down for changing in front and then one or more strides later behind (a late change). The horse will be marked down if he 'bunny hops' the change so that the new leading hindleg does not come forward enough, that is, both hindlegs step forward to the same point (so that the change is not 'through').

The flying change must be a definite, simultaneous spring from one pair of leading legs to the other. It is almost like taking a jump and, as in jumping, the rider's timing is vital. The aids for the change must be applied just before the moment of suspension in

Above Cindy Neale and Martyr are taking a good bound into the air when making this change of lead. This earns more marks than a change which is flat and therefore lacks 'expression'.

the canter (the only moment when he can change both forelegs and hindlegs). If the rider asks too early or too late, the horse will find it difficult to do more than change the lead of either the foreleg or the hindleg (depending on which is about to leave the ground), but not both.

Straightness

If a spectator watches carefully he will see good riders give the aid – a slight nudge with their leg behind the girth – just before the moment of suspension.

The problem of applying the leg behind the girth is that it tends to encourage the horse to swing his hindquarters to the opposite side. Hindquarters moving to the side of the new leading leg are a common sight, but not correct. Marks are deducted if the horse is not kept absolutely straight in the change.

Finn Larsen and Coq d'Or performing the most difficult of the flying changes, the one-time-changes every stride. The horse appears a little strong and keen to be going forward. The rider is having to hold him back strongly so that the horse is not in self-balance. The strides, however, are long and bold. In **A** he has just changed to the left lead. **B** is interesting because although he has changed freely in front on to the right lead the two hindlegs are together. This looks awkward and is described as a change not coming 'through' as the new leading hindleg has not been brought far enough forward. **C** shows clearly the moment of suspension when the horse is able to change to the left. Note the difference between this and the change to the right in **B**. In the latter case the new leading hindleg has come well forward to achieve a good, bold correct change.

A

B

C

D

A

B

C

D

E

Sarah Whitmore and Dutchman from Great Britain are doing a series of changes every few strides. In **A** they have just changed boldly on to the left lead. In **B** they are taking one of the interim strides between changes. His strides must have been becoming less collected for the head coming back to the vertical indicated she has applied a half halt. In **C** showing the moment of suspension when he makes the change, the horse has shortened up enormously. In **D** the change has come through and the rider has been able to release the rein pressure. In **E** he is taking a normal, pleasing interim stride.

Above Vol au Vent and M. Flament from France execute a free, forward-going change.

Expression

The other common fault is that although the change is made correctly, the stride is restricted, short and tense. As in all dressage work, freedom is important. The change should be light, bold and cadenced so that the period of suspension is pronounced. For this reason, slightly less collection is called for than in the normal collected canter. Good riders usually collect their horses prior to the change, by giving a half halt, and then ride them freely forward in the change itself. This helps to give the change 'expression', which is the 'icing on the cake'. A lifeless change may be straight, correct, light and fluent, but only those that have these features plus freedom and vitality (in other words, 'expression') will earn the highest marks.

Sequence changes

Most of the changes in the international tests are not simple single ones but series. In the latter the horse is asked to change either every fourth stride (four-time) or every third (three-time) or every second (two-time) and ultimately every stride (one-time). The difficulty increases the smaller the number of strides there are between. Thus in the Prix St Georges there are only 'three-time' and 'four-time', and it is not until the Intermédiaire II that the most difficult of all – the one-time – is first required.

The one-times look most striking to spectators – that slow, persistent rhythm of changing from one lead to another is spectacular to watch. They are, however, very difficult for both horse and rider to master. The rider has to be very precise with his aids and apply them with exact timing.

The horse must canter straight forward during the changes, for any swing to one side more than the other, or a muscle stiffness which limits the movement on one side, will have a cumulative effect that makes each successive change more difficult. In a long series of one-times the horse is likely to miss a change eventually because there is no time to restore balance, establish a better stride and get straight, as in the easier sequence changes.

The one-time changes require quick thinking and a great sense of rhythm from the rider, together with straightness, calmness, suppleness and impulsion from the horse. They are not easy and it is hardly surprising that so many mistakes are made – even by the best combinations.

Features	
Good	**Bad**
On the bit	Above/behind the bit
Stride long	Stride short
Correct	Late/not 'through'
Balanced, plenty of impulsion	Laboured or speeding up
	Swinging
Straight	Tense
Calm	Flat and dull
Expression	Rhythm changing
Fluent	Changes getting faster or slower and shorter or longer
Sequence	
Each change even	
Required number achieved	Changes missed

THE PASSAGE

In the passage the horse is as close as he can get to dancing. He has such control over his muscles and power in his body that he trots in slow motion and can still spring off the ground to produce that graceful prolonged moment of suspension. It is as if he were on springs. But the push off the ground cannot come from speed; it is solely suppleness and muscle power, and explains why the passage is so difficult to do well.

The aim

Ideally the horse should be very collected, with his hindquarters well engaged, his back supple and rounded, his neck raised and arched and his head close to the vertical. In this position he has the power to flex and spring off his hindlegs, and the lightness of the forehand to enable him to lift his forelegs exceptionally high in the air (the raised forefoot should rise to half-way up the cannon bone of the other foreleg, about one foot off the ground).

Levelness

The strides of the passage should abound with cadence and lightness and they must remain regular. The speed of the two-time rhythm is slower than that of the collected trot, so any irregularities become more obvious.

Many horses do not use their hindlegs with equal activity and this will show up in the passage with uneven time intervals between the hoofbeats of one

Above Uwe Schulten-Baumer and Slibovitz's passage may be less dramatic than Granat's but it comes easily. This is a pleasing picture and although it does not show so much flexion of the joints (the picture is taken at a later moment), there is an excellent lowering of the hindquarters, a nice rein contact, and the forelegs are a little higher than the hindlegs.

Above Christine Stückelberger's horse Granat achieves the passage of a gymnast rather than a ballet dancer. The strides have great spring and he is able to flex his joints to bring his legs high into the air. Often he is able to lower his hindquarters more than in this picture.

Above David Hunt and the German horse Marco Polo achieving a good passage. However, there is not so much lowering of the hindquarters as in the case of Slibovitz. As a professional rider David Hunt could not compete at the Festival so he acted as 'guinea pig' in the Grand Prix Special.

Above Amy-Catherine de Bary and Aintree are not performing their best passage. Aintree has hollowed his back, and his hindlegs have been left a little too far behind. The hindlegs are unable to create that vital impulsion from this position.

Above The British competitors Tricia Gardiner and Manifesto are capable of a very good passage, but in this case the horse has come above the bit which has made his outline slightly hollow. From this position it is difficult for him to engage his hindquarters sufficiently.

Above It takes great energy on the part of the horse to spring off the ground and to hold that prolonged moment of suspension needed in the passage. If he is feeling tired or truculent he will be less likely to co-operate. Cindy Neale seems to be having some trouble here with Equus, who is resisting by over-bending and is not lifting his legs far enough off the ground.

Above A lovely, springy, active passage performed by the Swiss competitors, but it is not perfect. The hindleg should not come higher than the foreleg, as it has done in this case.

pair of diagonals and the other. The passage is in such cases said to be unlevel, and this is a serious fault as the horse is not using one part of his body as much as another, and is close to being lame. This is usually due to muscle stiffness or weakness and sometimes 'bridle lameness' (in which the horse accepts one side of the bit but not the other, and this hardness on one side of the mouth is reflected in stiff muscles on that side).

In order to achieve the passage the rider must ask the horse to build up immense impulsion which instead of being released forward, as in extensions, is directed upwards to enable the horse to produce the elevated strides. Strong use of the rider's seat is vital to produce this impulsion, but he must apply it with great suppleness. Many riders find it difficult to absorb the exaggerated movement of the horse's back in the passage; they tend to stiffen, which makes the horse's back equally stiff. It is all too common a sight to see horses trying to passage with stiff, hollow backs and the hindlegs not engaged. Although they might keep each pair of diagonal legs in the air for a prolonged time there is little spring and cadence. The passage is flat and laboured. The grace and pride of the horse is lost in such a passage. In building up sufficient impulsion the horse

should not be made excited or tense, for then he will find it difficult to keep the same rhythm and take strides of equal length. Ideally, the general effect should be of calmness, fluency and elegance, with the horse finding it easy to produce this spectacular variation of the trot.

Features	
Good	**Bad**
On the bit	Above/behind the bit
Back supple and rounded	Back hollow and stiff
Hindlegs active and well engaged	Hindlegs trailing, and hardly leaving the ground
Level	Unlevel, hindlegs not used equally
Forelegs lifted to half-way up cannon, hindlegs to fetlock	Exaggerated action in front, little behind
Strides of even length, cadenced and light	Different-sized strides
Rhythm maintained, two-time pronounced	Flat, heavy strides
Straight	Changing rhythm
	Swings hindquarters and/or forehand from side to side

THE PIAFFE

The piaffe is the ultimate dressage movement used in tests, and as such is the most difficult. It remains beyond the capabilities of the majority of horses. Mastery of it is the distinguishing feature between a good dressage horse and a top-class dressage horse. A horse becomes more majestic and seems to grow in stature if, with talent and good training, he can learn to perform this trot on the spot with great collection, cadence and elevation.

To achieve good piaffe the horse must be more than a great athlete, he also needs great trust in and understanding with his rider. It is vital that he does not become tense and so lose his suppleness when, despite the driving aids being applied, he is stopped from going forward. The application of these two contradictory aids – urging activity and stopping forward momentum – is difficult for the horse to understand and he therefore tends to become tense. The rider is once again faced with the problem of balancing two contradictory features. He must build up sufficient energy for the horse to be able to take springy steps, but he must not make him so excited and tense that he loses his suppleness and, consequently, the ability to spring. The rider therefore needs great 'feel' (ability to anticipate and feel what the horse is doing and is about to do).

With these problems attaching to piaffe, many horses, even in a Grand Prix, do little more than shuffle on the spot or cheat by creeping forward. The exceptions, such as the World Gold and Bronze medallists Granat and Dutch Courage, can be breathtaking to watch, but they do not produce good piaffe immediately the rider presses the button. Even those horses that *do* have the talent and understanding of what is required have to be prepared mentally and physically, on each occasion, if they are to answer to the great demands of piaffe.

The aims

The horse should develop exceptional collection, lowering his hindquarters and springing actively off the ground with each of his hindlegs in turn; but only upwards, not forwards. The forehand must be light and free so that the forelegs can be lifted a few inches higher than the hindlegs (each foreleg should be lifted, as in the passage, to a height of half-way up the cannon bone of the foreleg, about 1 foot above the ground).

Above A classical piaffe by Vol au Vent: the hindquarters are well lowered, the limbs active, and the forehand light with the foreleg coming higher than the hindleg. Best of all, it looks easy.

A

B

C

D

E

Uwe Schulten-Baumer asks Slibovitz to piaffe in **A**. Perhaps he asked too strongly or perhaps the horse was lacking sufficient engagement of the hindquarters to enable him to trot on the spot, for, sadly, in **B** Slibovitz has not been able to lift a diagonal pair of legs. He has only raised a foreleg. By **C** he has lifted the required hindleg and is now lifting a foreleg without its diagonal hindleg – i.e. he has lost the trot and failed to keep the diagonals needed for piaffe. By **D** he has picked up the rhythm and shows how piaffe should be performed, but cannot maintain it. Perhaps the fore- and hindlegs have come too close together for the horse to keep his balance, as in **E** all four feet are on the ground. This sequence illustrates how difficult it is for even the great combinations to achieve piaffe at the spot demanded. All the basics of dressage (impulsion, submission, rhythm, talent, etc.) must combine together in just the right degree, at just the right moment, to achieve good piaffe.

The horse should retain the true diagonals of the trot, that is, lifting the diagonal foreleg and hindleg simultaneously. Only then can the purity of the pace with its pronounced two-time rhythm be maintained. He must use his hindlegs equally, too, otherwise the hoofbeats will be irregular and he will have an unlevel piaffe.

The neck should be held gracefully high and arched, and the head vertical. The rein contact should be light but constant, and this is only possible when the horse is in a good balance and therefore not reliant on the reins for support. When in such a balance it will be easier for him to lift his legs high into the air and still return them to the same spot. In the piaffe the appearance should be of harmony – the entire body working and co-ordinated. Thus those vital back muscles must remain supple and working freely, with the back rounded, not hollow and stiff.

Faults

Many horses have to struggle to produce these steps on the spot, and in their efforts produce unattractive side-effects. Some cross their forelegs, swing their forehand and/or hindquarters from side to side or, worst of all, step backwards. Although the horse remains on the spot in piaffe, that vital desire to move forward must not be destroyed or even hindered. Backward steps are therefore serious faults.

Impulsion

The piaffe should result in a build-up of power from the extra engagement of the hindquarters, and this should be instantly available for use whenever the rider wishes to go forward. This power is developed if there is spring and cadence to the steps of the piaffe, with the horse swinging easily from one diagonal pair of legs to the other. With good piaffe

Above A very satisfactory piaffe in which the horse Satchmo is clearly lifting his diagonal pair of legs. For the higher marks, however, the hindlegs need to be more engaged and the limbs lifted higher; but this takes great talent, suppleness and power to achieve.

Above It is quite common to see a piaffe like this one, where the hindleg is lifted higher than the foreleg. It will not earn higher marks as the hindquarters are not lowered and the forehand is not so light.

Above Anne-Marie Sanders-Keyzer and Amon have been consistently placed in international classes for many years. Amon appears relaxed in this piaffe and is in good self-carriage with a light rein contact. He is using his foreleg well but his diagonal hindleg is a little lazy.

Above Christine Stückelberger and Granat's great success is due in part to their consistently good piaffe, a movement which earns a high percentage of marks in a test. Although this is not an example of his best piaffe it is still very good. The foreleg is lifted to the desired level, higher than the hindleg. The hindquarters are not so well engaged as this Swiss partnership usually manages.

the rider is in control of a great power which is submitting happily to his will; when this is achieved, it feels very good to the rider and looks very good to the spectators.

Many people tend to confuse impulsion with speed, but more impulsion is needed to produce good piaffe than for any other movement; yet the horse should not be moving forward – the speed is 0 mph. Impulsion is contained energy, and that is what the horse needs in an immense quantity if he is to do good piaffe.

Use in tests

The piaffe is first required in the Intermédiaire II, but in an easier training form. Seven or eight piaffe steps are to be made when moving forward through one metre. Each step is therefore a few inches forward, which makes it slightly easier to develop the impulsion, for the strides to be cadenced and elevated, and to make the horse understand and to keep him relaxed. In the Grand Prix, more steps of piaffe are required (ten to twelve) and they should be performed on the spot. Only the top combinations seem able to produce cadenced, regular piaffe on the spot.

Features	
Good	**Bad**
On the bit	Above/behind the bit
Rein contact constant and light	Pulling/no contact
Forefeet lifted to half-way up cannon bone on other leg; hindquarters lifted to fetlock of other hindleg	Flat, shuffling steps
	Back hollow and stiff
	Horizontal outline or hindquarters higher than forehand. Hindlegs not engaged
Back round and supple	
Hindquarters lowered and well engaged.	Unlevel, hind- and/or forelegs used unequally
Level	Loss of two-time rhythm
Rhythm maintained with simultaneous lifting of a diagonal pair	Swinging forehand and/or hindquarters; crossing legs
Straight	Steps backwards, lazy, no power
Great impulsion and forward desire	Laboured, stiff, tense
Movement harmonious, supple and easy	

THE TRANSITIONS

There are more transitions in a test than in any other type of movement. The competitor is constantly making them within paces (from collected to medium, extended to collected, etc.) and from one pace to another. For the judge, the standard of these frequent transitions is one of the major considerations when marking. Some transitions are considered so important that they have a mark to themselves. The latter include the transitions in that tricky movement when competitors halt, rein back X number of strides, forward Y, back Z and then into trot or canter (as in Intermédiaire I and Intermédiaire II). The halt, rein back and advances are therefore allotted a maximum 10 marks, and the transitions a further 10.

The most difficult transitions of all, from piaffe to passage and vice versa are considered so important that they earn 50 marks in the Grand Prix: that is, each of the five transitions in and out of piaffe and passage has a possible mark of 10. These are in addition to separate marks awarded for each section of piaffe and passage.

In theory, these transitions between piaffe and passage should be made without altering the rhythm, but it is very difficult to keep sufficient impulsion in the piaffe to make this possible. All too often the cadenced strides of the passage are lost as the rider asks his horse to produce his strides on the spot. This leads to a break in the rhythm, but the high percentage of marks given for transitions in the Grand Prix and the Grand Prix Special means that the competitors pay heavily for such a weakness.

It is in these transitions that horses like Granat earn their marks and make up for obvious mistakes in the changes, or the odd explosion. Granat has such impulsion, and yet such control, that he can move fluently and rhythmically between the two most advanced dressage movements to accumulate many good marks.

These transitions in and out of piaffe and passage are a test of the most important factors in dressage – impulsion, rhythm, fluency, submission and suppleness. This is the reason for the high proportion of marks allotted to transitions in international tests.

For the spectators, it can be confusing. Mistakes in the changes are obvious, but a slight stiffening and loss of rhythm in the transitions, although less discernible, will lose many more marks. This is because poor transitions prove a lack of talent and correct training. Missing a change is usually the result of a slip in the rider's timing or a momentary loss of concentration. This is a far less serious error and consequently it is less heavily penalized.

A

B

C

M. Flament and Vol au Vent's downward transition at arena point A into the collected trot does not start as well as it ends. In **A** the rider is applying the seat (he is a little behind the perpendicular) and the legs to engage the hindquarters. The hindquarters, however, have come a little high and the horse has fallen momentarily on to his forehand so that he becomes heavier in the hands. By **B** this has been corrected for he is now in a good outline, light in the hand, and the rider has come back into the upright position which he maintains in **C**.

A

B

C

Above An upward transition from trot to canter. In **A** Vol au Vent is still trotting but in **B** the body outline has been compressed. The rider must have applied a half halt in preparing the horse for the next pace. In **C** the body outline has lengthened again as he takes his full canter stride.

Above Jane Bartle and Landmark from Great Britain make the transition from medium to collected trot. The rider is using her seat and legs to encourage engagement of the hindquarters, but the horse has stiffened.

Dressage marks are distributed in a manner which determines the best trained and most talented competitor, and not according to the ease of understanding for spectators. Transitions are one of the best tests of good training and are therefore the source of a large percentage of the marks in a test.

The aim of transitions

The aim should be to make the change of pace or speed at the stated marker smoothly yet distinctly. The horse should remain light, calm and on the bit. The rhythm of the pace is maintained up to the moment when the pace is changed or the horse halts.

In a similar manner to collecting, the horse should be ridden forward into downward transitions. It is vital that the hindquarters are engaged and that the seat and leg aids are applied prior to the rider using a restraining, but allowing, hand. If the energy is retained, the horse is less likely to stiffen his back and resist than if the rider simply pulls on the reins.

Features	
Good	**Bad**
On the bit	Above/behind the bit
Hindquarters engaged	Hollow back, hindlegs dragged
Impulsion maintained	
Rhythm maintained	Impulsion lost
Fluent	Rhythm changed
	Abrupt

THE SALUTE AND EXIT

The test comes to an end with the horse halting and the rider saluting. In the easier tests (from the Prix St Georges to the Intermédiaire II), the competitor canters down the centre line, halts, reins back and canters off to halt close to the judges at G.

This movement tests straightness and contains many of the requirements discussed under 'The Entry'. There are also such additional factors as checking whether the horse reins back straight and moves off into the canter directly without swinging his hindquarters. Any deviations are detected immediately as three judges are straight ahead.

In the Grand Prix and the Grand Prix Special an even more difficult approach is required. The horse has to passage down the centre line and then go smoothly into piaffe before halting. Any of those all-too-common swings from side to side of the hindquarters and/or forehand are easily detected. Tests are devised so that the judges will have the opportunity of seeing movements from all important angles. The important piaffe and passage are therefore viewed from the side and from straight ahead during the test.

Whatever the approach to the final salute, the horse should halt smoothly and stand square. Most riders try to give the judges a happy, relaxed smile to show that they enjoyed their test. Then the horse and rider can relax after a gruelling ten minutes or so on show. As they walk out of the arena on a long rein it is not possible for any ambitious rider to be contented. In dressage it is impossible to do everything right: mistakes are always made, and movements can always be performed better in this sport. Dressage is the pursuit of perfection.

Contentment might be out of reach upon completion of a test; pleasure and exhilaration, however, are not. These can be felt if some movements were performed better than expected, if the horse worked to or above his usual standard, or if he was trying his hardest and the ride was harmonious.

The fact that there will always be weaknesses to criticize in a test, that it could have been done better, should not detract from the high spots, the parts that felt and looked good. Competitors, if they are to be happy, must be aware of the weaknesses but nevertheless derive pleasure from the good points. More important, the rider should relay happiness and gratitude to his partner, who, it is hoped, has stretched his ability to the maximum just for him.

The gratitude and the happiness were much in evidence when Christine Stückelberger saluted the judges after her breathtaking performance in the Grand Prix Special at the Festival. Granat was given every possible form of appreciation by his rider. In those moments, the rapport between that great combination was obvious, and the pleasures that dressage can give both horse and rider were gleefully apparent on that occasion.

Below Reiner Klimke makes his salute on Ahlerich. The horse remains on the bit. It is almost a square halt, but the off hindleg is just a few inches too far back to be perfect.

Above It is all over, and Christine Stückelberger gives her great horse Granat a long rein and a pat as a reward for his exceptional performance in the Grand Prix Special. **Above right** The international tests are very long and demanding. David Hunt and Marco Polo look quite exhausted after their efforts. **Below** Anne-Marie Sanders-Keyzer looks happy and rewards Amon after a good performance.

At the end of all the tests come a few minutes of glory for the successful combinations. Throughout the competition scores will have been displayed on the board and each of the five judges' totals given; the final score is the addition of these. The combination with the highest total is the winner; it is the winning

horse and rider who lead the prizewinners out to their positions in front of the grandstand to listen to their national anthem being played and to see their country's flag being raised.

These are moments when pride is allowed to show, when the years spent searching for a talented

Top Competitors and spectators scrutinizing the scoreboard. **Above** One of the colourful trappings of victory is the music of the band.

Above The team champions from Germany (Uwe Sauer, Uwe Schulten-Baumer and Reiner Klimke) canter out of the arena with their spoils of victory.

horse, the even longer time spent in training and the sacrifices involved in having to ride and train almost every day of the year earn high rewards.

In dressage, these egotistical moments of glory are not such a driving force as, for example, in show-jumping. They occur only rarely, even for the top competitors. Each horse is capable of keeping his spirit and *joie de vivre* only for about six international shows a year. The travelling and the highly demanding build-up, requiring exceptionally concentrated work for one to three hours a day prior to the test, cannot become a regular routine. For a horse to achieve his best performance he may need up to

two hours' riding, which entails great physical and mental strain for the horse.

Then there are those long tests in which more than ten minutes are spent in the arena, a period when every aspect of the horse's body control and suppleness is tested: these require great fitness. In dressage there is not the same endurance strain as in eventing, but there are plenty of other strains. This means that a dressage horse rarely lasts at international level for more than two or three years unless his international appearances are limited.

Fortunately for the dressage rider, there are many sources of pleasure other than the prizegiving, and even competitions. The competition is the test that proves that the work at home has been done correctly, and also provides the driving force to do this training.

Where dressage wins over other sports is that the training itself is challenging, fascinating and, on occasions, very satisfying. The dressage rider is fortunate in that not only are there moments of glory for those who ride to the top but the path towards this goal is full of rewards, pleasures and fun.

Above The champions line up for their individual medals after the Grand Prix Special. The prizes were presented by Britain's Prime Minister, the Rt Hon Mrs Margaret Thatcher.

Above Lady March and the Countess of Inchcape congratulate Christine Stückelberger.

THE FINALE

International competitions have a number of important bonuses for participants. Competitors are not only given a wonderful opportunity to travel and to meet many important people in foreign countries, but they are also provided with an unique opportunity to get to know and understand people from other nations. Indeed, with the common bond of a sport – and even better, the horses themselves – language and cultural barriers are quickly broken down.

In addition, through international competitions dressage riders have the chance to find out not only about the training methods and riding techniques used in different countries but also about life abroad in all its aspects.

To further these beneficial side-effects and to enable the host country to show hospitality, social gatherings have become an important aspect of international competitions. Goodwood is renowned for its lavish hospitality. Its ballroom, an elegant room lined with works of art, was the scene of a magnificent ball held for the Festival competitors –

an occasion which must have placed Britain high in the popularity ratings and promoted a great deal of international camaraderie.

Competitors need to relax to be able to take the enormous strains of international competitions. During the competition this is possible mainly in the evenings – around the stables, at parties or over dinner. But no competitor can completely rid himself of tension until the finale. Only when it is all over can the riders lose the strain of knowing that unless they make the greatest possible effort they will have wasted a very special opportunity.

Not all the competitors will reach the show's finale happy with their results and glowing with the pride of having done well and been publicly recognized for their performance. Nevertheless the competitive atmosphere always has the effect of inspiring participants to ride better and train harder in the future. As for the prizewinners, they will leave in the happy knowledge that their hard work and dedication has been justly rewarded.

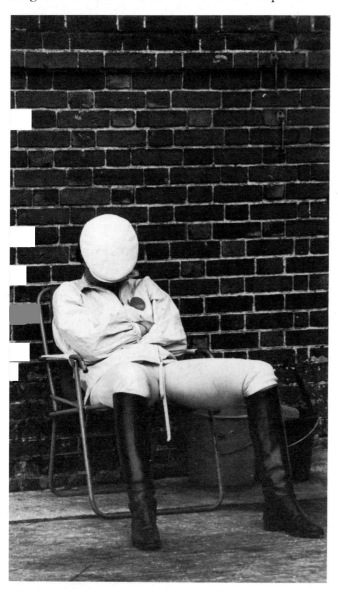

Above and right The competition over, some riders catch up on sleep while others relax with a beer.

Top Floodlit Goodwood House, looking magnificent. **Above** Inside the house there is a splendid dinner and dancing for competitors, owners, organizers and helpers at the Festival.

Below Time to go home.

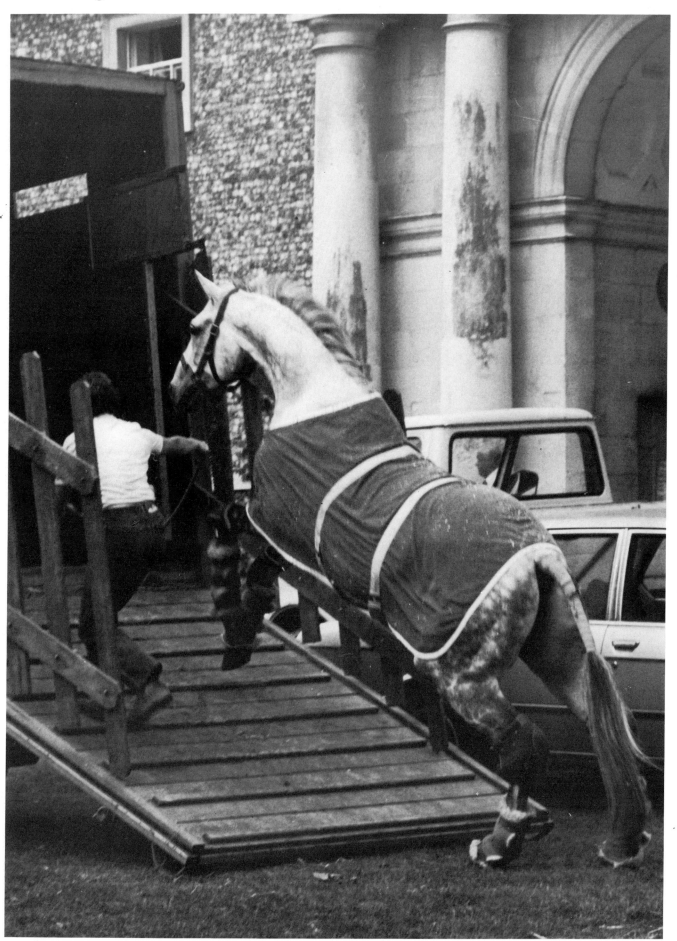

GLOSSARY

Arenacraft Experienced riders, with a touch of showmanship, are able to show off their horse's ability to best advantage in the arena. Important features of arenacraft are: to ride deep into the corners to give horse and rider more room to manoeuvre; to show distinct differences in the paces; to ride accurately, and never to throw points away unnecessarily.

Balance Ability to maintain a good rhythm, take even strides and remain on the bit – all of which make the horse more able to do the movements well.

Bit *Above the bit:* the horse is not 'on the bit' but trying to evade the rein contact by carrying his head too high. His nose will be in front of the vertical. His back is likely to stiffen and even to become hollow. *Behind the bit:* this is the opposite fault to being 'above the bit'; the horse draws his head inwards with his nose coming behind the vertical. It is another way in which horses try to avoid rein contact. *On the bit:* see 'The Test', page 50.

Cadence Pronounced rhythm and energy in the pace.

Collection Achieved by engagement of the hindlegs [forward] under the horse's body, enabling the horse to take shorter and higher steps. The head and neck are raised to form a harmonious curve from the withers to the ears. The poll (the point just between the horse's ears) should be the highest point, and the head should be slightly in front of or on the vertical. The collection is poor if the steps become shorter but remain flat (i.e. no elevation) and/or the hindquarters are not engaged: in both cases impulsion will be lacking. Collection is one of the major objectives of dressage, for when a horse is collected he becomes more manoeuvrable and balanced; he is also a lighter and more pleasurable ride. In collection the horse will find it easier to carry out the most difficult movement in dressage tests –piaffe, passage and canter pirouettes. The amount of collection a horse is capable of achieving depends upon his stage of training (Prix St. Georges horses show less collection than Grand Prix horses), his natural ability and how well he has been trained.

Crooked/not straight In all movements, except lateral work, the horse's hindlegs should follow in the tracks of his forelegs. If the hindquarters swing to the inside (very common at the canter), or if he halts with his hindquarters to one side, the horse is said to be crooked. It is a serious fault to be more than momentarily crooked, as it leads to uneven muscular development and makes it difficult to collect a horse or to build up impulsion.

Disunited The horse canters with a different leading leg in front from behind, thus making the sequence of the pace incorrect. It becomes either off hindfoot, near hindfoot and near forefoot, and finally off forefoot, or near hindfoot, off hindfoot and off forefoot, and finally near forefoot.

Forehand The horse's shoulders, front legs, neck and head are known collectively as the forehand. When most of the weight falls 'on the forehand' the hindquarters cannot be engaged, which makes it difficult to develop impulsion. When the forehand is heavy there is also a lack of lightness and mobility, causing the horse to be less manoeuvrable and less balanced. To be on the forehand is a serious fault.

Forging When the toe of the hindfoot shoe hits the heel of the forefoot, making a noise this is known as forging. It is a fault.

French terminology The French led the development of dressage during the seventeenth, eighteenth and nineteenth centuries and gave names to many dressage movements, which are still pronounced as in French, e.g. piaffe, passage, renvers and travers.

Grinding teeth A form of resistance (*q.v.*), and marks are deducted when this occurs

Half halt Achieved by applying the aids to halt but releasing them before the horse does so. It is a means of collecting the horse and warning him that something is about to happen. See 'The Entry', page 62.

Hindquarters *Engaged hindquarters:* when the horse puts his hindlegs well under his body, using them actively and showing good flexion of the joints. This engagement is vital to develop impulsion and good collection. *Hindquarters leading or trailing:* this refers to horses in the half pass when, in the former, the hindquarters are ahead of the forehand, or, in the latter, have been left behind. Both are faults, because the horse should be almost parallel to the long side with the forehand just in the lead.

Hurrying Starting to rush and thereby losing rhythm.

Impulsion Contained energy created by the activity of the hindquarters, which enables the horse to go forward. See 'The Test', pages 54–5.

Late change Said to occur when, in the flying change, the horse does not change his front and hind lead legs simultaneously. It is more common for a horse to be late behind when he changes in front and then one or two strides later behind.

Lateral movements Those requiring sideways as well as forward motion.

Leg yield The horse is straight in this movement except for a slight bend at the poll away from the direction in which he is moving. The horse's legs on the side of this slight bend pass and cross in front of the legs on the side of the direction of the movement. This movement of the legs is similar to that in the half pass. It is the easiest of the lateral movements, requiring no collection. It is not included in the international tests.

Near side/leg Sides/legs which are on the left.

Off side/leg Sides/legs which are on the right.

Outline The silhouette of the horse's top line, from his ears to his tail. A round outline (convex) to the neck and the back is good, a hollow outline (concave) is bad. Advanced horses are expected to have a shorter outline than novice horses.

Overbent The horse is overbent when his nose comes behind the vertical as he bends his neck, bringing his head too close to his chest.

Resistance Not accepting the aids of the rider. This can include the horse throwing his head in the air, opening his mouth, crossing his jaw or hollowing his back.

Square halt See 'The Entry', page 64.

Strides *Flat:* with little or no suspension in the sequence. The horse will be less manoeuvrable, and without the flexion of the joints there will be less impulsion. *Running:* going too fast, with quick, unbalanced strides. *Irregular:* the rhythm of the pace becomes irregular, and one or more strides are in a different rhythm to those before and after.

Uneven: the strides are of different lengths. *Unlevel:* taking unequal strides with both the hindlegs or both the forelegs.

Tilting head The nose is raised and turned to the left or right so that the head is on a slant to the right or left. This is a form of resistance.

Track When on 'one track', the hindfeet follow in the footsteps of the forefeet. In lateral work the horse is on two or more tracks.

Vertical A line perpendicular to the ground from the horse's forelock to his nose. The nose should not come behind the vertical; it can be on or in front of it in collected work and should be distinctly in front of it in the extended paces.

Working paces A trot or canter between collected and medium which is required of horses not ready for collection. It is therefore used in the novice and easier tests but not at international levels.

Wrong bend When turning corners and in all lateral work, except leg yielding, the horse should have a slight bend in his neck and body. The direction is specified and if this is not established then the horse has the wrong bend.

SEQUENCE OF PACES

Dressage is a system of training the horse to develop his natural abilities. No dressage movement demands anything that a spirited young horse would not naturally do when playing in a field. The emphasis in training is that the work should be natural to the horse, hence the importance of maintaining and improving the natural paces of the horse. Purity of paces is a vital aspect of correct training, and in dressage tests any deviation from the natural sequence of the paces is severely marked down; the trainer should never spoil what is natural to the horse. For each of the three paces – the walk, the trot and the canter – there is a correct sequence:

At the walk four hoofbeats are heard at equal intervals apart, in this order: left hindfoot, left forefoot, right hindfoot and right forefoot.

At the trot two hoofbeats are heard with the legs moving in alternate diagonal pairs with the hoofbeats separated by a moment of suspension: right forefoot and left hindfoot together, then left forefoot and right hindfoot together. The moment of suspension is when all feet are in the air.

At the canter three hoofbeats are heard and, as in the trot, there is a moment of suspension when all four hooves are off the ground; e.g. when the left forefoot leads the right hindfoot hoofbeat is followed by the left hindfoot and right forefoot together then the left forefoot and finally the moment of suspension. When the right forefoot leads, the left hindfoot hoofbeat is followed by the right hindfoot and the left forefoot together, then the right forefoot and after this the moment of suspension.

PICTURE ACKNOWLEDGEMENTS

The author and publishers wish to thank the following for permission to reproduce photographs:
Central Press Photos, page 11 *below left*; Cooper Bridgeman Library, page 13 *below*; Mary Evans Picture Library, pages 9 *below* and 10; Trustees of the Goodwood Collection, pages 12 *above*, 13 *above* and 15 *below*; Michael Holford, page 8 *below*; Illustrated London News, pages 14 and 15 *above*; Keystone Press Agency, page 11 *below right*; Mansell Collection, page 9 *above*; National Portrait Gallery, London, page 12 *above*; Colonel A. Podajsky, page 11 *above left*; Sally Anne Thompson (Animal Photography), pages 16, 17, 29, 31, 33, 38, 39 *above*, 40–41, 42, 48 *above and below*, 136 *above*, 138 *above*, 139 *above* and jacket; R. Willbie (Animal Photography), pages 34, 35 *above and below*, 36, 37, 39 *below*, 43, 44 *above and below*, 45, 46 and 47.

All other photographs in the book are by John Bunting.